Computer-Assisted Instruction for Students at Risk for ADHD, Mild Disabilities, or Academic Problems

Computer-Assisted Instruction for Students at Risk for ADHD, Mild Disabilities, or Academic Problems

Renet L. Bender
Truett-McConnell College

William N. Bender
University of Georgia

Allyn and Bacon
Boston   London   Toronto   Sydney   Tokyo   Singapore

Copyright © 1996 by Allyn & Bacon
A Simon & Schuster Company
Needham Heights, Massachusetts 02194

Library of Congress Cataloging-in-Publication Data

Bender, Renet Lovorn.
    Computer-assisted instruction for students at risk for ADHD, mild disabilities,
or academic problems / Renet Lovorn Bender, William Neil Bender.
        p.   cm.
    Includes bibliographical references and index.
    ISBN 0-205-16062-X
    1. Computer-assisted instruction—Handbooks, manuals, etc.
  2. Handicapped children—Education—Handbooks, manuals, etc.
  3. Computer managed instruction—Handbooks, manuals, etc.
  I. Bender, William N.   II. Title.
  LB1028.5B433   1996
371.3'34--dc20   95-36332
                                                                                 CIP

Printed in the United States of America
10 9 8 7 6 5 4 3 2 1   00 99 98 97 96

*To my parents, Jackie and Tom Lovorn,
with loving thanks for their support
and guidance through all the years.*

Contents

1

Introduction

Renet L. Bender

Upon completion of this chapter you should be able to:
◆ *Identify uses of the sections in this text.*

In their classrooms, teachers are almost always expected to teach students at varying levels. This is particularly true in the inclusive classrooms of today. The proper use of computers and computer-assisted instruction (CAI) can be of considerable help to teachers in this and other instructional settings. The use of CAI can assist master teachers in totally restructuring their methods of instruction. For example, if a student with a disability needs more work on spelling than other students, the teacher may utilize CAI to assist this student. The student would receive the individual attention he or she needs to keep up with the rest of the class, and the teacher would have more time for individualized lessons with other students. The benefits of CAI include not only significantly enhanced learning for students (Dailey & Rosenberg, 1994; Higgins & Boone, 1990; Keyes, 1994) but also more job satisfaction for the teacher.

This book is written as a "How To" guide for the integration of computers and CAI in the classroom. It is intended for teachers at all grade levels whose classrooms include students who are at-risk or students with mild and moderate disabilities. However, the suggestions presented here have been used successfully with students at all ability levels. Furthermore, the book includes information and suggestions for teachers at all levels of computer literacy. The only requirement is that the teacher knows how to turn on his or her computer and how to handle a floppy disk.

The main goal of this book is to help teachers achieve total integration of CAI in their classroom. The authors divide this goal into small tasks, each of which can be accomplished in a short amount of time, approximately 10 to 20 minutes. Added together, these tasks allow teachers to achieve the goal of total integration of CAI. At all times we have been mindful of the needs of teachers and students in the classroom setting. The importance of the individual at-risk student is stressed throughout. We have been careful not to overload you with unnecessary technical information but to give practical classroom suggestions. In writing this book, it is our intent to help teachers with their work, by making suggestions that give good results and that can be done in small increments of time. Each of the chapters is self-contained, which allows you to select the topics in which you are most interested.

This book has been structured to have several uses. It can be used by individual teachers as a "How To" guide, as previously mentioned. It can also be used as a reference guide for teachers who have extensive experience using CAI. For example, we give useful information on the different types of educational software that is now available and provide suggestions for using the software in lessons. We discuss how to obtain information on computer programs that fit the needs of all students. We include examples and suggestions on using computers to make paperwork manageable. Moreover, we discuss some of the newest teaching methods that utilize computers.

We have also structured this book to be used as an effective resource for in-service teachers. Each chapter is written so that it can be used as the basis for an in-service program, lasting from two hours to half a day. All chapters also include specific activities or steps intended to help teachers achieve the goal of the chapter. Before each activity, we state the objective of the activity and invite you to skip over it if you are familiar with the objective.

We have organized the manual into seven chapters and three appendices. Chapter 2 discusses learning characteristics of students, including students with mild disabilities. We look at how the attributes of computer programs can help students, given their particular learning characteristics. In addition, we present the types of computer instruction available. Chapter 2 also includes a discussion of the use of computers as reinforcement.

Chapter 3 identifies the information that teachers must know about their computers to purchase computer software. Instructions for obtaining this information are included in the chapter. Special equipment that is required for some programs to run properly is identified and discussed. In these discussions, we include price ranges, information on where to find the product, and installation procedures. Chapter 3 also guides teachers through evaluating computer programs for use in their classrooms. Forms are included in the chapter to assist in this task.

Three important issues are addressed in Chapter 4: using computers in the classroom, instructional options for the classroom, and teaching students the types of technology that they will use in the workplace. Discussion on the use of computers in the classroom focuses on three topics: placement of computers, scheduling of computer time, and teaching students to use computers. Suggestions are included for helping students to be self-reliant when told to use a particular program on the computer. These suggestions include successful techniques for nonreading students. The section on instructional options for the classroom includes effective instructional principles, integration of CAI, and lesson options (modifications that teachers can make to computer programs to individualize them for particular students). The third major issue discussed in this chapter addresses the types of technology that students are expected to use in their daily lives and gives suggestions on incorporating this technology into classroom lessons.

Chapter 5, written by Gary Ross and William Bender, focuses on computer-managed instruction. The chapter is intended to help teachers reduce their amount of paperwork through the use of computers. Computers can be used to keep track of attendance, grades, and student performance, as well as to generate report cards, letters to parents, and individualized education plans (IEPs). Three sections in Chapter 5 discuss classroom management, IEP generation, and behavior support. In each of these sections, we review several computer programs that can help teachers in these tasks. Suggestions on how the programs can be used are also made.

Multimedia, discussed in Chapter 6, is one of the newest technologies. It is a combination of several different types of media linked together by a computer and produced for viewing on the computer screen. Multimedia typically combines audio, text, videotape, print, and graphics in one presentation. The most exciting attribute of multimedia is the ability of the user to easily change from one topic to another and to change media at any time. The attributes of multimedia are presented in Chapter 6, along with a general discussion of how it works and the advantages and disadvantages of using multimedia with students. The chapter also includes examples of how teachers can use multimedia, some examples of multimedia software, and steps to evaluate multimedia software.

Chapter 7 examines several ways in which teachers may use CAI to enhance and improve their teaching skills. In particular, this chapter concentrates on the effects of professional improvement for the master teacher. We include recommendations on dealing with burnout, strategies for professional improvement in computer-assisted instruction, and suggestions on how to obtain money and support for CAI implementation ideas.

This book also includes three appendices that contain information that will be useful to many teachers. Appendix I contains a description of software mentioned in the book; Appendix II is a list of software sources; and Appendix III contains descriptions of hardware that is popular with all students but especially so with students who are physically disabled.

To reiterate, our goal in writing this book is to help teachers fully integrate computers and CAI in their classrooms. This will help at-risk students and others learn better, and will give teachers more time to spend with individual students.

References

Dailey, E. M., & Rosenberg, M. S. (1994). ADD, Computers & Learning: Using Computers to Help Children with ADD Become Efficient Learners. *Attention!*, 1(2), 8–16.

Higgins, K., & Boone, R. (1990). Hypertext Computer Study Guides and the Social Studies Achievement of Students with Learning Disabilities, Remedial Students, and Regular Education Students. *Journal of Learning Disabilities*, 23(9), 529–540.

Keyes, G. K. (1994). Motivating Reluctant Students: The Time on Computer Program. *Teaching Exceptional Children*, 27(1), 20–23.

2

What Computers Can Do

Renet L. Bender
William N. Bender

Upon completion of this chapter you should be able to:
- *Identify learning characteristics of at-risk students that suggest CAI applications.*
- *Identify computer attributes that aid instruction.*
- *Name the types of CAI.*

Computers have many uses in the classroom for at-risk students and students with mild disabilities. For example, computers may be used to introduce new material using graphics, words, and sound to hold a student's attention. Computers may be used for independent practice on any type of repetitive task in spelling, language arts, mathematics, or any other area. Computers may be used for simulation activities to put students into situations that, in the real world, would be dangerous. In fact, the range of uses of the computer is almost limitless (Boysen, 1994).

In this chapter, we will explore the use of computers and computer-assisted instruction (CAI) for several specific types of tasks, including initial instruction, practice, simulations, and problem solving. We will also discuss using computers to motivate students, and using computer tools—such as word processing—to help students complete assignments. You will be amazed at the many uses of computers for students with mild disabilities. You will also be impressed with the quality and quantity of software now available for these students. However, computer use is both a privilege and a responsibility. With the growing use of computers, and the increasing amount of high-quality software now available, comes the responsibility for teachers to have a high level of computer skills in order to utilize computers appropriately (Caftori, 1994).

In this chapter, we discuss the characteristics of students with mild disabilities that make the application of computer-assisted instruction particularly useful with this group. Further, we look at the types of computer instruction available for students with learning difficulties.

Characteristics of Students in Need

Almost all mainstreamed students with mild disabilities may benefit from the use of computers in their educational programs. Students who are identified as emotionally/behaviorally disturbed, learning disabled, or mildly mentally retarded demonstrate a particular set of learning characteristics that suggest that they can often benefit from use of CAI programs. Further, children without disabilities who may be at-risk for learning problems, such as students with attention deficit hyperactivity disorders or students in Chapter I federal programs in reading and math, may also benefit from CAI. When at-risk students are combined with students with mild disabilities, these students constitute from 12 to 20 percent of the students in the mainstream classroom. For our purposes, in this book we will refer to all of these students as *at-risk students*, since they are all at risk for learning problems.

This book is intended to address computer technology and its successful use for these at-risk students. Although we will not cover computerized adaptive technology for students with low frequency impairments in depth (use of this technology is discussed in Appendix III), we will discuss the skills necessary for efficient use of CAI. Efficient use of CAI by teachers should benefit not only students at-risk but every student in the class.

Let's look at how you can efficiently use CAI with your students by considering the needs of at-risk students. The two activities, Try This 2.1 and 2.2, are designed to help you identify common learning characteristics among your students. If you are familiar with the characteristics of your class you may wish to skip these activities.

> ***Try This 2.1*** *List the characteristics of students at-risk and students with disabilities in your class. Think of one or two specific students and list their learning problems, in terms of their attention span, classroom behavior, task persistence, and attitudes toward learning. Compare these lists to identify common characteristics. You may use Form 2.1.*

FORM 2.1

Characteristics of My Students

Attention Characteristics:

1. How long will this student concentrate or work on a task at his or her functional reading level? _____

    _____

    _____

    _____

2. How frequently does this student complete assigned worksheets in class?

    _____

    _____

    _____

3. How often does this student not turn in homework? _____

    _____

    _____

4. What other attention behaviors have you noted? (Describe a particular example.)

    _____

    _____

    _____

Memory Characteristics:

1. Does this student have problems remembering concepts from one day to the next?

    _____

2. Does this student have problems remembering things from a few minutes ago? ____

    _____

3. If yes to questions 1 and/or 2, what kinds of things does the student forget? _____

    _____

4. Are repeated lessons necessary for this student? _____

    _____

5. Describe an example of poor memory by this child. _____

    _____

Behavior Characteristics:

1. Does this student exhibit disruptive behavior in the classroom? _____

    _____

2. How frequently do you have to discipline this student? _____
   _____
   _____

3. The last time you had to discipline the student, what was he or she doing? _____
   _____
   _____

4. Describe one or two examples of this child's misbehavior. _____
   _____
   _____
   _____

Subject Variations:

1. In what subjects is this student strong? _____
   _____
   _____

2. In what subjects is this student weak? _____
   _____
   _____

3. Identify particular types of tasks that this student cannot do (seatwork, attention to lectures, discussions, etc.). _____
   _____
   _____

Academic Modifications:

1. Is this child on grade level in reading, math, and language arts? _____
   _____
   _____

2. What modifications are necessary in your teaching to allow this child to succeed?
   _____
   _____
   _____

3. What other modifications do you think would work? _____
   _____
   _____
   _____

Now let's work through this completed Form 2.1 together. As a prompt, ask yourself questions about the students' work habits. For example, how long do they stay on task on a worksheet? What implications does this hold for educational planning on computer drill and practice exercises? How long should these exercises be?

> ***Try This 2.2*** *Most students with mild disabilities exhibit some or all of the characteristics listed on Form 2.2. You may wish to name the specific students in your class who demonstrate these characteristics.*

With these characteristics in mind, you must now consider appropriate instructional techniques. These characteristics suggest a number of learning problems that may require specific instructional modifications. The modifications may include the need for step-by-step elaboration of tasks, the need for models of task completion, the need for concrete examples, and the need for shorter assignments. You should add additional modifications to address the other characteristics mentioned. Of course, the salient point is that each of the instructional needs presented here can be met through effective use of CAI software, without taking up a great deal of your instructional time.

As you begin to enhance your skills in CAI, you must consider the needs of individual students as the primary basis of software selection. Your second concern must be implementation of CAI within the content of effective instructional principles (Vockell & Mihail, 1993; Malouf, Jamison, Kercher, & Carlucci, 1991). These principles are presented and discussed throughout this book. The two activities you just completed were intended to show the relationship between the needs of at-risk students and the types of instruction necessary for these students. Always remember: When considering CAI applications, you must begin with students' needs, rather than merely using the available software.

FORM 2.2

Characteristics Displayed by Specific Students

Common Characteristics	*Students Who Demonstrate These*
1. Low frustration level	_____
	_____
	_____
2. Lack of interest	_____
	_____
	_____
3. Short attention span	_____
	_____
	_____
4. Easily distracted	_____
	_____
	_____
5. Short- and long-term memory recall problems	_____
	_____
	_____
	_____
6. Different rates for learning the same content	_____
	_____
	_____
	_____
7. Variations in subject strengths and weaknesses	_____
	_____
	_____
	_____
8. Poor fine motor coordination	_____
	_____
	_____
9. Overlapping disabilities	_____
	_____
	_____

CAI, Effective Instruction, and Student Learning Characteristics

CAI can assist in each of the instructional modifications mentioned in the previous section (step-by-step elaboration of tasks, models of task completion, concrete examples, and shorter assignments) and other modifications. For example, the rate of presentation of information and response times on CAI can be varied, or are self-paced, and this allows the student great flexibility in work completion. Pacing, or the speed of the introduction of problems during a lesson, is a major concern in structuring efficient instruction for at-risk students. Further, most computer software can be easily sequenced and broken down into small steps for instruction. This allows the teacher to plan shorter assignments for students with short attention spans, without interrupting the ongoing instruction for other members of the class.

CAI can excite students and motivate them to get work done. For example, students may view math or spelling on a computer as fun, whereas they may be reluctant to do the same task on a worksheet. This reinforcement characteristic of CAI instruction makes this teaching technology extremely useful. In this sense, using a computer can be viewed as a reward for good behavior.

Further, efficient CAI use can improve a student's attitudes toward learning. When a student makes a mistake, the computer tells the student he or she made an error, without any emotional pressure or embarrassment. This subtle and timely feedback will greatly enhance a student's learning. Thus, the student is likely to experience less frustration and a higher level of success, and this often results in improved attitudes toward school in general.

Using a computer also offers the opportunity to practice eye-hand coordination, a skill some at-risk students find difficult. Furthermore, modern CAI software uses sound and graphics to help keep students on task. For example, when using software that teaches students addition, the software may use dancing figures to give the answer to the addition problem. Not only do figures dance but they may also sing a song when the student gives the correct answer, or a correct series of answers. This is highly rewarding and leads to improved attention skills.

Software for at-risk students also calls for numerous responses. This allows for more practice opportunities than traditional worksheets. Increased exposure, along with the immediate feedback CAI offers, will increase achievement.

Finally, CAI can be used either one on one or in a group. This management flexibility will assist you in time management of the busy mainstream, special education, or inclusive class. The activity in Try This 2.3 helps you to identify attributes of computer software and match them to the learning characteristics of your students. If you have already been doing this in your class, you may wish to skip this activity.

> ***Try This 2.3*** *Choose a computer program that you use in your class and use Form 2.3 to identify the attributes of this software. For example, these attributes will include varied response times, graphics, or auditory reinforcement.*

FORM 2.3

Attributes of Computer Software

1. Does this software allow you to change the response time for the student?_____

   _____

   _____

2. Does this software have a high level of repetition?_____

   _____

   _____

3. Does the student receive immediate reinforcement for correct answers? _____

   _____

   _____

4. Does the software use graphics and sound adequately to help keep the student on task?

   _____

   _____

5. Can this software be used in time lengths appropriate for this student? _____

   _____

   _____

6. How many questions in sequence are presented? _____

   _____

   _____

7. Does the software instruct the student to get teacher help? _____

   _____

   _____

8. How does the software deal with an incorrect response? _____

   _____

   _____

9. If the student gives an incorrect response, does the software review the student on the material or keep recycling over the questions the student has missed? Which do you prefer?

   _____

   _____

10. What other software characteristics are important to you? _____

    _____

    _____

TABLE 2.1 *Matching Students' Characteristics and Computer Attributes*

Students' Characteristics	*Computer Attributes*
Low frustration level	Variable response times High repetition Immediate reinforcement
Lack of interest Short attention span Easily distracted	Use of graphics and sound Frequent reinforcement
Short-and long-term memory recall problems	Variable response times Frequent repetition Use of graphics and sound
Different rates for learning the same content	Variable response times

Table 2.1 matches the attributes seen in Form 2.3 to the learning characteristics in Form 2.2. Two characteristics of at-risk students are not addressed in Table 2.1. Variations in academic strengths and weaknesses is dealt with by the software chosen at specific academic levels. This issue will be addressed in Chapter 3. The other characteristic, poor fine motor coordination, will be discussed in the section on how to teach students to use a computer in Chapter 4.

Types of CAI

History of CAI Development

When computers were first introduced into the classroom, teachers had a tendency to use computers as a reward for good behavior and to use computer worksheets modeled after traditional paper and pencil worksheets. As a result, the first types of programs that teachers purchased were usually either drill and practice software or games to be used as rewards. With the drill or independent practice programs, teachers had a tendency to plan lessons around the computer software rather than the students' needs. The programs that were then available were not particularly flexible and were similar to the paper and pencil worksheets used in many traditional lessons. These games and electronic worksheets did not truly explore the range of possible computer applications. Further, teachers realized that regular worksheets were more affordable and easier to use, and schools could not justify the expense of computers when they were used exclusively in this manner. Finally, because of the low quality of software, many people who used these software applications were dissatisfied and may have abandoned classroom applications of the computer altogether.

Fortunately, the number of computer applications has now expanded into a wide range of possible uses. CAI is currently available for instructional activities ranging from initial instruction to mastery assessment. Furthermore, software companies have become aware of the needs of at-risk students and are producing a larger quantity and better quality of software for these students.

We will discuss seven types of computer instruction in this book. Class management and student assessment software will be discussed in Chapter

5. In this chapter, we will introduce the other five types of CAI, which include initial instruction, mastery practice, simulations, problem solving, and the use of computers as tools. As you look at these five types of CAI, you should think about how you can use each of them in your class.

The first two types of CAI, initial instruction and mastery practice, assist the teacher in teaching content material in basically the traditional manner. The primary advantages of these two types of CAI are freedom for more creative teaching and more time with individual students.

The second two types of CAI, simulations and problem solving, use new and different ways of teaching. They are used to introduce the student to new learning experiences at a more global, synthetic, and applied level.

Instructional Software

The first two types of computer instruction that we will talk about, initial instruction and mastery practice, are similar in that they allow the teacher to use the same methods of teaching that they have always used. However, they free the teacher to help other students or to teach more creatively. In other words, unlike in traditional teaching, the teacher does not have to be immediately present when students use these types of CAI software.

Initial Instruction

One effective use of CAI is introduction of new material. Initial instruction (sometimes known as direct instruction) consists of five basic components (Vockell & Mihail 1993): (1) setting clear goals for students and making sure the students understand these goals; (2) presenting a sequence of well-organized lessons; (3) giving students clear, concise explanations of the subject and subject matter; (4) asking students frequent questions to determine if the students understand the work; and (5) giving students frequent opportunities to practice what they have learned. As we discussed earlier, CAI software is well suited to this task. Software of this nature is designed to introduce content material to the student, to assess the student's understanding, and to provide reinforcement based on the student's responses. This software is not designed to take the place of the teacher totally, but rather to work with the teacher in the presentation or the representation of new material to the at-risk student. As a result of the belief that the teacher should introduce the student to new concepts, very little software may be considered solely as initial instruction.

Initial instruction software usually presents the new material in written and graphic form, and questions the student repeatedly throughout. If the student responds to a question incorrectly, these programs go back to that material and review it or repeat the exercise in a different format.

At this phase of the learning process, computers have several attributes that are helpful. Computers consistently present the student with the overall idea as well as the subconcepts, thus giving the student not only the pieces but also the connections between facts and concepts. Further, computers can present concepts in graphic, written, and auditory formats simultaneously, and this multimodal presentation of the same information to different senses can strengthen the student's understanding. In fact, many at-risk students seem to progress more academically in such a multimodal curriculum. This type of presentation may also interest the student more and thus help keep him or her on task.

During initial instruction, computers give immediate feedback, and research has consistently shown that immediate feedback enhances learning. Also, CAI offers several pacing options, and the pacing—the rate of introduction of new problems—can usually be modified by the teacher to meet the needs of the student. For example, *Words and Concepts* by Laureate Learning Systems, Inc. (Apple II series, Apple IIGS, Macintosh, IBM, and IBM compatible computers) is a software package that can be used as initial instruction to introduce vocabulary words to students. (All software distribution companies discussed in this text are listed in Appendix II.) It also is a mastery practice program in that it "trains" the student in the meaning of the words, categorizes the words, and helps the student with the concepts of same and different.

Words and Concepts consists of six programs covering the content areas of vocabulary, categorization training, word identification by function, word association, concept training—same, and concept training—different. Vocabulary, as one example, presents 40 nouns to the student in two sets of 20. Each noun is presented by a picture with the word written underneath the picture. When each noun is presented, the program speaks to the student, saying, "This is a———." The student is immediately shown three nouns on the screen, in the same word and picture format. The student is asked by the program to select the noun that was previously introduced. Correct responses are reinforced. The other programs work with the student on the different concepts mentioned previously, using the words introduced in the vocabulary program.

Whenever a program is selected in this CAI package, the teacher is given the option of changing parameters via a parameters menu. Pacing is one of the parameters that can be varied in this software program. The teacher can change the number of seconds the program waits for the student to respond before moving on to the next presentation. The response time can be set between 1 and 10 seconds.

Most of the six programs comprising *Words and Concepts* have an errorless learning feature built in. Errorless learning involves structuring the academic lesson to eliminate, as nearly as possible, the possibility of the student making an error. This increases student success and facilitates mastery. In this CAI package, three levels of difficulty are available. All three levels provide reinforcement or corrective feedback depending on the student's response. For Level 1, a visual prompt (an arrow) appears over the correct answer. In Level 2, the visual prompt appears only after the student misses a question. In Level 3, there is no visual prompt.

The teacher is also able to preselect the number of questions the student must answer correctly in order to proceed to the next skill level. Also, the teacher can stop the student on a particular level. The program will start the student on level one and progress to the level specified by the teacher. This is important because teachers can prevent the student from moving to a skill level for which he or she is not prepared. A more detailed discussion of this CAI software and others can be found in Appendix I.

As seen in the preceding example (and in Appendix I), effective CAI gives the teacher control over an extensive number of parameters. These parameters include pacing of the program, terminal behavior, the type of feedback the student receives, and immediate reinforcement. The most effective CAI programs have errorless learning features built in. The parameters listed here should be considered when choosing initial instruction software, since these parameters partially determine how well the software can be integrated into the curriculum.

Mastery Practice

A large part of students' learning time is spent in guided and independent practice. While early CAI software was performing these tasks in classrooms 10 years ago, the software for guided and independent practice has improved remarkably.

After being presented with new topical material, the student usually requires practice with frequent feedback as the next phase in the typical learning process. Traditionally, this is done in two ways. First, teacher-guided practice takes place immediately after initial instruction, when the teacher guides the student through several problems. Then the student is typically assigned to do a series of problems independently, as either classwork or homework. Use of CAI can eliminate the distinction between teacher-guided practice and independent practice because the CAI program can guide students toward errorless practice. This frees the teacher to work with other students or to do other tasks. For this reason, we have chosen to use the term *mastery practice,* since CAI blurs the traditional distinctions between the guided practice and independent practice phases of learning.

Mastery practice software usually has a repetitive overlearning capability that is extremely useful with at-risk students. Normally, the teacher would be responsible for ensuring that students practice new material until a performance level is reached that allows for independent practice. Typically, when a student can complete 75 percent of the problems correctly, he or she is ready to move from guided practice to independent practice. CAI, however, moves the student to independent work immediately, usually in some errorless learning format. Of course, the teacher should be careful to monitor the student's progress in one of the several ways mentioned in Chapter 5. Still, the computer is quite effective in mastery practice instruction because the computer is patient. Also, the computer will wait for an answer, quietly correct errors with an appropriate review of the content material, and reward the student for each correct answer. These CAI advantages make the computer extremely useful for mastery practice.

For example, *Number Munchers* by Minnesota Educational Computer Corporation (MECC) (Apple, Macintosh, IBM, and IBM compatible computers) has a game-like format in which animated characters eat numbers or math problems that meet certain specifications. One area of practice involves multiples of numbers. The multiples game consists of 30 squares on the screen, each containing a different number. At the top of the screen the student is told what multiples to find. For example, the student may be asked to find multiples of 2. The student moves an animated character, the number muncher, around the screen, and selects answers by pressing the space bar to make the muncher eat the numbers that are multiples of 2. To make the game more interesting, there are other animated characters—Troggles—that try to "eat" the number muncher or change numbers in the squares. In addition to giving students practice on multiples of numbers, *Number Munchers* also offers practice on factors of numbers, prime numbers, and simple math problems involving equalities and inequalities.

In this program, the pacing automatically increases as a student progresses through the games. The pacing is determined by how fast the Troggles move around the screen; the faster the Troggles move, the faster the student must make selections to identify correct answers. The game automatically starts at the lowest level and increases as the student progresses.

After successfully completing three games, the student is rewarded by a short cartoon. If the student makes an error, the computer makes a horn sound and tells the student to look again. After four errors on a screen, the program stops that game and asks the user if he or she would like to play again. In this case, there is no reward and the level of play does not increase.

MECC gives you, as the teacher, a number of options in this program. For example, you have the option of preventing students from playing any other particular game.

In *Number Munchers*, the student may play a game where the screen consists of 30 squares, each square containing a different addition problem similar to "10 + 5." The objective is for the number muncher to eat the squares that contain problems that give the same answer as the answer at the top of the screen. The teacher is allowed to restrict answers to a certain range and to specify if the answers are to appear in random order or in increasing order. This CAI software is discussed in more detail in Appendix I.

Summary

Initial instruction and mastery practice software utilize the same methods that teachers use to teach content material to students and to review students on that material. These two types of CAI have several characteristics in common.

First, they do not require the student to solve very complex problems. In a software program that gives the student practice in addition, the program will ask the student for an answer, provide limited feedback, and reinforce the student for correct answers, but it does not involve role-playing or sophisticated problem solving.

Next, the sequence of almost everything that the student sees on the screen is predetermined by the CAI program. In other words, the student must follow the sequence of the CAI program. The student either gives a correct answer or a wrong answer, and the CAI software responds with either a guided example or with the presentation of another problem. This contrasts rather dramatically with multimedia software described in Chapter 6.

Finally, both initial instruction and mastery practice software depend mainly on rote memory. Skills in problem solving and brainstorming to generate new problem solutions are not strengthened by this type of CAI.

In some CAI software for mastery practice, differences are apparent between software intended for guided practice and independent practice software (Malouf, Jamison, Kercher, & Carlucci, 1991). While such a distinction is not common, you should consider the attributes of the software relative to the intended purposes. CAI software that is to be used for the guided practice component of mastery practice should have remedial feedback, an unhurried pace, repeated occurrences of missed items, an errorless learning feature, and facilities for teacher monitoring.

The software for the independent practice component of mastery practice exercises should have a quick response rate and numerous motivational reinforcers. Also, an escalating feedback feature should be included (i.e., a CAI program feature that increases the quality and quantity of feedback for the same or similar types of errors). This escalating feedback feature will allow the student to learn from his or her mistakes, even in the absence of direct assistance from the teacher. Finally, variable pacing should be built in, such that as a student makes fewer errors, the program pace automatically speeds up.

Applications Software

The next two types of computer instruction involve application of knowledge; they include simulations and problem solving. Both types of instruction use nontraditional methods of teaching content material and problem solving to expand the students' learning experience, and they provide realistic practice in complex applications of knowledge. These types of software go beyond the traditional phases of learning to help the student participate in real-world applications of knowledge, as modeled on the CAI software. Thus, these two types of computer instruction require the student to use cognitive skills and to practice real-world decision-making skills, in the applications of knowledge and judgment.

Simulations

Simulations are software designed to re-create social, political, and historical systems, and to make the student an active participant in those systems. Simulations allow students to participate actively in situations that may not be safe or feasible for them to do in the real world. For example, chemistry simulation programs allow and encourage students to experiment with mixing different substances together. In an actual laboratory, this would be impossible due to the threat of explosions resulting from a wrong mixture. However, by using a simulation, the students can see, without harm to themselves or anyone else, what happens if they mix the wrong chemicals together.

Simulations can offer an inexpensive way to facilitate informal learning for students. For example, *Oregon Trail* by MECC (Apple, Macintosh, IBM, and IBM compatible computers) is a simulation of the pioneers migrating west on the Oregon Trail. Along the way, participants actively engage in roles that involve deciding what supplies to purchase, when to make camp, when to continue traveling, where to cross rivers, and so on. For example, when starting the program, the student is asked to choose a profession. Choices of professions include a doctor, a carpenter, a farmer, and others. Based on the profession chosen, the student is informed of the amount of money he or she will have for the purchase of supplies.

During the journey, the student is required to make decisions about when to rest, continue the journey, ford rivers, purchase more supplies, hunt, change the speed of travel, and change trails. Bad decisions usually result in illness, injury, or possibly death to the character portrayed by the student or to another member of the party. The student is rewarded for consistently good decisions by safely completing the journey.

To plan and carry out such a major expedition is impossible for most people, due to cost and time requirements. But a simulation, such as *Oregon Trail*, encourages some of the informal learning that would take place on such an adventure. This simulation would work well with groups of students or with an entire class. The students must have reading skills to read the instructions and information presented during the journey. The school version of *Oregon Trail* comes with student handouts and an easy-to-read manual.

Simulations may also be used to speed up or slow down events, thus allowing the student the opportunity for more learning experiences. For example, a simulation of an ecosystem will show the effects of a drought on that system in a matter of seconds rather than days, months, or years.

Some of the newest forms of simulation software are programs to teach the student life skills. One example is the *Skills for Living Series* by Hartley (Apple, Macintosh, IBM, and IBM compatible computers). *Skills for Living* is a simulation package that teaches the student several important skills for living in today's society. It consists of 10 different programs, each teaching the student a new skill. Instruction in life skills of this nature is particularly appropriate for at-risk students.

One of the programs in this series is "Checking Accounts." In this program, the student is taught the skills used to manage a checking account, including checkbooks, deposit slips, and bank statements. Another program, "Comparison Shopping," helps the student learn how to comparison shop. In this program, the student "goes" to a grocery store with a list of items to be purchased. The student must make purchasing decisions, taking into account unit price, value, and coupons. Other programs in this simulation package are discussed in Appendix I.

There are a number of advantages in the use of simulations.

1. Simulations encourage students working in groups to achieve goals.
2. They allow students to experiment by trying alternatives.
3. Skills that are learned on simulations may be more readily transferred to the real world.
4. Simulations allow the asking of "What if" questions, which are not entirely appropriate in lecture situations.
5. Simulations allow students to be put into situations that might be dangerous in real life.
6. Simulations help students increase their learning experiences.
7. Simulations can be a very effective cooperative learning method. Teachers should use this type of CAI to assist in the integration of children with disabilities into all instructional groups in the inclusive mainstream classroom.

When using simulations, there are several possible disadvantages.

1. Simulations require time. A simulation activity may not fit into a single class period; the activity may stretch into several days or weeks. Most simulations come with lesson plans to aid in planning for this longer time frame for instruction.
2. As with all software, teachers should not believe everything the manufacturer says with respect to the goals of the software. For example, most simulation software claims to teach the student problem-solving skills and reasoning skills that will benefit the student in all areas. As will be seen later, problem-solving and reasoning skills are difficult for students to transfer from one area to another.
3. Students can easily turn a simulation into a competitive situation. Teachers should monitor the students and encourage cooperation and collaboration between students, rather than competition.
4. Students with mild disabilities may have difficulties in playing roles in the simulation software, and the teacher will probably need to work with these students to teach them these skills. Figure 2.1 gives several suggestions for helping at-risk students understand the concept of role-playing.

The use of simulations in the classroom may be best understood in terms of four phases: preparation, supervision, debriefing, and evaluation (other writers have suggested other categorizations; Horn & Cleaves, 1980; Willis, Hovey, & Hovey, 1987).

FIGURE 2.1   Role-Playing Techniques

1. Discuss the role-playing as a pretend game. For example, you could say to the student, "Let's pretend you are a farmer." In the context of the role, discuss the types of actions or things the farmer would say.

2. Specifically teach the role by modeling the types of statements a student in that role would likely say.

3. Tell the student that other students will also be playing roles.

4. During the second day of simulation activity, again teach the concept of role-playing by additional modeling of the role and/or by having the other students model their roles.

5. At the conclusion of the activity, review all the roles.

Preparation involves selecting the simulation, making adaptations, and integrating the software into the curriculum. For example, to select the software, you could use the school media center or software catalogs. Most simulations come with lesson plans as a guide to teachers. Teachers should use these suggestions to adapt the simulation to fit their curriculum, and discard those that do not fit. By using a few of the first lesson plans provided, you can decide what changes, if any, need to be made for the simulation to be integrated into your curriculum.

Supervision depends on the simulation chosen and the students' level. For example, as mentioned earlier, some students may need help in role-playing. The teacher's role may be as involved as actively playing a role, or it may be as minimal as playing troubleshooter for the simulation activity. As the students gain more experience with the simulation, supervision usually shifts to a more supportive, low-key role.

Debriefing involves discussing the issues dealt with in the simulation and helping students go over the concepts and processes they learned in order to draw closure. The teacher should also take the opportunity to discuss the differences between the simulation and the real world. The debriefing could be used as a springboard to other concepts you wish to introduce on the same topic. This is a crucial aspect of simulation use, because the restatement of concepts at this point greatly enhances learning.

The evaluation phase involves evaluating the effectiveness of the simulation software. You need to decide if the simulation helped to accomplish the desired objectives. If the software is used again, are there any changes or modifications that you would make in order to make the simulation more effective? Finally, what did the students think of the simulation? You should always include input from the students; they can usually provide numerous suggestions for improvement. Evaluation of software prior to purchase is described in the next chapter.

Problem Solving

In most classrooms, teachers concentrate on teaching students factual knowledge. Teachers give the students lectures, worksheets, and exams, hoping that as a result of acquiring this factual knowledge, the students will be able to solve problems. Presently, not enough instructional time is given to complex problems or the development of the skills to solve problems. Problem-solving software can help you by teaching students problem-solving skills while not subtracting from the amount of time you spend on factual knowledge. Next, we will discuss the types of problem-solving software available and give suggestions for teaching problem solving.

Types of Problem-Solving Software

Problem-solving software can be classified into two categories: subject specific and nonsubject specific. Subject-specific problem-solving software is what most people think of when problem solving is mentioned. This type of problem-solving software presents problems in a specific context, subject, or content area, such as mathematical problem solving. Occasionally, simulation software may fall into this category. Nonsubject-specific problem-solving software is intended to assist the student in learning higher-order thinking skills. Such skills may include analysis, synthesis, and evaluation of alternate solutions to a problem.

Subject-Specific Software.   There is a variety of subject-specific problem-solving software. One example, *Math Blaster Mystery* (Apple II series, Macintosh, IBM, and IBM compatible computers) by Davidson, uses the format of a mystery game to help the student learn how to do word problems and prealgebra. *Math Blaster Mystery* has four activities, each with four levels of difficulty. One of the activities, called "Follow the Steps," teaches the student how to solve word problems. In this activity, a word problem is presented and the student is asked to answer four multiple-choice questions. The first question asks the student to identify the type of answer necessary (i.e., what the problem is asking the student to find). The second question requires the student to consider what information is needed to solve the problem. The third question requires the student to select the correct formula to use in solving the problem. The fourth question asks the student to select the correct answer. Repeated practice using these four questions should greatly enhance a student's ability in problem solving.

These questions represent the four basic steps in problem solving, which can be transferred to many types of problems. However, research has indicated that many students never learn these simple steps. *Math Blaster Mystery* emphasizes these four steps when solving problems. With each step, the program gives the student immediate feedback. For example, when the student answers a question correctly, he or she may be told that the answer is correct. When the student misses a question, the program first uses an errorless learning feature. It does this by highlighting the correct answer and the portion of the problem that pertains to the problem-solving step being presented. One disadvantage in this program is that if a student continues to miss the question, the Apple IIe version tells the student to look again and does not proceed. We recommend that the student should be instructed to summon the teacher if he or she misses a question three times. This will prevent the student from remaining on the same question for the entire computer time.

All the activities in this CAI program have four levels. For example, with "Follow the Steps," Level 1 contains problems with one or two operational steps using addition, subtraction, multiplication, and division with whole numbers. Level 2 has problems with one or two steps using operations with whole numbers, fractions, and decimals. Level 3 contains two-step problems using all four math operations with fractions, decimals, percentages, ratios, and proportions. Level 4 contains problems with two and three steps that involve percentages, decimals, and fractions used in combination.

In addition to "Follow the Steps," *Math Blaster Mystery* includes several other activities. "Weigh the Evidence" challenges students to develop strategies to move a set of weights from one scale to another, given certain rules. "Decipher the Code" helps students to develop higher-order thinking skills as they discover a mystery equation. "Search for Clues" requires students to try to find a mystery number by searching for clues in a room full of objects and characters. In this activity, students learn that there are many ways to describe and define a number. More details about this CAI package can be found in Appendix I. A newer version of *Math Blaster Mystery,* called *The Great Brain Robbery* is available for computers with Windows and CD-ROM.

Another example is *Math Shop Jr.* by Scholastic. *Math Shop Jr.* portrays a mall, consisting of 10 shops, in which the student works. The student can work in one of the shops or in all 10 at the same time. Each shop requires a different set of skills, and each customer wants something slightly different. This CAI software is also discussed further in Appendix I.

Nonsubject-Specific Software. The second category of problem-solving software is software that teaches students general problem-solving skills. For example, *Call the Parrot* by Hartley (Apple II series computers) teaches younger students the ideas of north, south, east, and west, and how to take notes. *Memory Match* by Hartley (Apple II series, IBM, and IBM compatible computers) encourages careful observation and thinking, whereas *Glowy* by Hartley (Apple II series computers) teaches critical thinking skills for addition, subtraction, and whole-number concepts. *Perplexing Puzzles* by Hartley (Apple II series and Macintosh LC computers) teaches students to think logically, to read more critically, and to question what they read. *The Great Space Race* by Hartley (Apple II series and Macintosh LC computers) is an interactive program in which students hone their problem-solving abilities by using a model, gathering and interpreting data, and making assumptions by "assembling" a rocket engine, testing the engine, and then competing in a race to the moon.

One CAI software package that teaches general problem-solving skills is *Where in the World Is Carmen San Diego?* by Broderbund (Apple II series, Macintosh, IBM, and IBM compatible computers). With this software package, the student plays the role of a detective and tries to solve crimes. For example, in one game, an art treasure has been stolen and the student is told to solve the crime by a certain deadline. To aid the student in solving the crime, he or she can choose from four categories to find information. One category is "Connections." This is a list of the cities that are destinations of direct flights from the city of the crime. The investigator may then leave the city of the crime and arrive at the city of his or her choice from the Connections list. "Investigate" presents the student with a choice of three places to investigate. Each time the student investigates a site, he or she is given more clues to the crime (if the student is on the right track). "Interpol" results in the student entering data in Interpol's computer and receiving a list of suspects. While the student is investigating, each activity takes time and results in the student getting closer to the deadline. A more detailed discussion of this software is found in Appendix I.

Carmen San Diego has been used in schools across the country and is well known for its ability to help teach students the art of problem solving. When using problem-solving programs, students may become disappointed in themselves when they fail to solve a problem. In situations like this, the teacher should spend time with the student at the computer observing the student and how he or she goes about solving problems, and then work with the student to enhance problem-solving skills.

Developmentally Appropriate Problem-Solving Instruction

Adapting instruction based on the different cognitive developmental levels of students is necessary for lower-level at-risk students. This type of instruction is referred to as developmentally appropriate instruction. CAI use can assist the teacher in such adaptations.

Bloom's taxonomy gives the developmental stages of cognitive thinking (Sprinthall & Sprinthall, 1990). The six stages are as follows:

1. *Factual Knowledge:* Factual knowledge involves gathering or learning facts in content areas. There is a great deal of software available for this developmental stage. For example, *Words and Concepts* (reviewed earlier) helps the student with vocabulary and spelling.
2. *Comprehension or Understanding:* Aside from gathering or memorizing facts, students must understand the facts they have learned. It is easy to assess the students' mastery of content material by testing. Depending on the content area, the amount of software available for testing students varies. For example, there is a large amount of software for testing in the areas of spelling and math but comparatively little in the areas of music or history.
3. *Application of Skills:* In addition to gathering knowledge and understanding that knowledge, the student needs to be able to apply that knowledge where applicable. However, it is difficult to assess skill application in some content areas. For example, in math, the teacher could test for application skills by using word problems. In English, the teacher would ask the student to write a paper. However, in other content areas, such as political science or introductory psychology, testing application of skills is more difficult.
4. *Analysis of a Solution:* Given a solution to a problem, the student must be able to use his or her knowledge to analyze the solution. It is often difficult to determine if the student has achieved this skill on worksheet types of tasks. However, simulation software is excellent for this, since it presents problems and possible solutions to the student.
5. *Synthesis of a Solution:* At this developmental stage, the student is given a problem and must find a solution. This skill is extremely difficult to measure. Usually, measurement is done by working closely with the student and observing this process. Here again, simulation software can be useful.
6. *Evaluation:* After the synthesis of a solution to a problem, the student needs to be able to evaluate that solution. This is usually done by observation. Simulation software can be useful for this also.

Maddux, Johnson, and Willis (1992) suggested that teaching problem solving should involve all six of these stages. Further, the nation's educational effort could be strengthened considerably by more concentration on these diverse, articulated stages. Due to the cognitive developmental stages of students in the schools, the first three stages are typically the main emphasis for students at elementary school levels, whereas the last three are stressed more in the secondary schools. The problems with this approach are obvious. First, to learn the last three stages, the student must have mastered the first three stages, and many at-risk students have not completed this task by the end of elementary school. Also, the later tasks should receive more emphasis earlier in the curriculum to better prepare students for secondary subjects.

CAI, when used to teach problem solving, can assist the teacher in identifying the appropriate developmental level. Most CAI problem-solving programs have several levels built in, and the student's initial answers will help in determining the level of work for later problems.

We recommend the following considerations for using problem-solving software:

1. For students functioning in the lower- to middle-elementary level, the first three stages should be emphasized. Yet some time should also be spent in higher-order developmental skills. For higher-functioning students, all six stages of problem solving should be taught, with emphasis on the higher stages.
2. Subject-specific problem-solving software should be chosen over non-subject-specific problem-solving software whenever possible. Problem solving involves the ability to obtain knowledge and to use this knowledge. Furthermore, research by Krasnor and Mitterer (1984) indicates that it is extremely difficult for students to transfer general problem-solving skills in one subject to another subject. Consequently, non-subject-specific software, intended to teach indistinct things such as "thinking skills," is probably not very effective in teaching at-risk students to generalize these skills across subject areas.
3. Nonsubject-specific problem-solving software may be used if the objective is to change a student's attitude toward problem solving, or if the specific skills taught by the software are the skills that you want to teach. For example, the *Call the Parrot* CAI program described earlier should be used if you are specifically interested in teaching directional skills of north, south, east, and west.
4. Plan adequate time for problem-solving learning to take place. Do not expect an at-risk student to master problem solving of any type in one CAI session. Rather, plan a series of brief (10 to 15 minutes) CAI sessions over a period of days to move toward mastery. At-risk students will take longer to master these tasks than students without learning problems.
5. Plan for group use, on a cooperative basis, of CAI that involves problem solving. You should attempt to subtly influence the group interactions toward positive interactions that involve students with and without disabilities.

Summary

Simulation and problem-solving software utilize new and better methods for teaching content material to students. These two types of CAI have several characteristics in common.

Both types of computer instruction generally involve active, intellectual involvement from the student. Not only will the student complete a task from rote memory but he or she will also be actively involved with the task. This student-task interaction is an important advantage of applications software over the more traditional types of CAI.

The student has control over his or her interaction with the computer and what happens on the screen. Again, the student is an active participant in learning. Also, simulation and problem-solving software call for more creativity from the students than initial instruction or mastery practice software.

The teacher needs to be aware, however, that simulation and problem-solving software require hours of use before the user has seen everything the software has to offer. Therefore, good evaluations on these two types of software are difficult to find.

The next activity is designed to help you take inventory of your problem-solving and simulation software. You may wish to skip this activity if your classroom lacks this type of CAI software at present.

> **Try This 2.4**   *Use Form 2.4 to list and classify your problem-solving and simulation software.*

Computers as Tools

Computers as Reinforcement

During all phases of learning, motivation of at-risk students is an important consideration, but this is a crucial concern during the early phases. From the students' perspective, computers are still relatively unique in many mainstream and special education classrooms. Therefore, they can be used as a motivator for some students if appropriate software is selected.

Reinforcement Options

There are three types of "motivation" activities. First, computers can be used as a reinforcement for appropriate behavior when the teacher rewards the students by allowing them to choose the game they wish to play on the computer. For example, you may be pleased with a student's behavior and decide to reward that student by allowing him or her to play on the computer with any software the student chooses. Of course, the student may pick a game that has absolutely no educational value whatsoever, but reinforcement is the goal, and a few minutes on the computer can be very reinforcing.

The second type of motivational activity is reinforcing the students by allowing them to choose the type of educational software they wish to use from selections that are identified by the teacher. In this instance, the student is allowed to use the computer, but he or she must use an educational program, such as a program for math, writing, or even a simulation package. Here, the reinforcement value of the CAI is still available, but the student is also learning while he or she uses the computer.

The third type of motivation activity is using the assets of the computer to integrate technology into the student's curriculum, so that the student becomes aware of the benefits of this technology. Clearly, this is the most desirable reinforcement use of the computer. For example, word-processing software is a useful classroom tool that will motivate many students (MacArthur, 1994). Students who have difficulty with spelling and grammar quickly learn that they can successfully use word-processing packages to produce a finished letter or paper, often in less time than writing it by hand.

Word-processing software also allows for ease of production and revision. When the student writes, the teacher usually collects the paper, corrects it, and hands the paper back to the student for revision. Many students find this grading/revision process somewhat punishing. CAI can eliminate this painful aspect of revising an unfinished product. Furthermore, word-processing software eases the physical requirements of writing. With word processing, students spend more time on composing rather than on the actual mechanics of

FORM 2.4
Problem-Solving and Simulation Software

Software	Type	Specific Skills Taught	Prerequisite Skills (reading/math level)

writing. This is certainly an advantage for "slower-to-write" at-risk students or for students who may acutely fear the writing process. Finally, research has shown that word processing helps to change students' attitudes about writing, resulting in more positive attitudes toward writing and school in general (Daiute, 1986; Montague & Fonseca, 1993).

Integrated CAI

Use of multisensory software can be useful for students who are easily distracted or have short attention spans. You may recall from an earlier activity that many at-risk students with learning problems have attention problems. Also, the use of graphics can help a student who has difficulty with short-term or long-term memory since graphic presentations of data are more easy to remember. A spelling activity on a worksheet, in which a student may not be interested, can be turned into an exciting task using CAI.

Students can start word processing at an early age. For example, *Kid Works 2* (IBM compatible computers with or without Windows and Macintosh computers), by Davidson, motivates students by allowing them to illustrate their writing with colorful pictures; the program also reads the words to the students. Figure 2.2 is an example of an illustrated story created using *Kid*

FIGURE 2.2 *An Illustrated Story from* **Kid Works 2**

I live on a farm. We have horses, pigs, and cows. They live in a big red barn.

Works 2. The program combines a word processor, a paint program, and text-to-speech technology (which reads the words to the student), allowing students to express themselves. It can be used by students at the prereading level through advanced reading levels.

Kid Works 2 has four activities: "Story Writer," "Story Illustrator," "Story Player," and "Icon Maker." "Story Writer" gives students a computer screen that looks like a piece of primary writing paper. The student can quickly learn to change fonts, select pictures, choose icons to represent words, and select speech from the options menu to hear a word or group of words read aloud. For more advanced writers, the computer screen can be changed to appear as a ruled piece of writing paper. The student can save his or her work, edit an earlier story, or delete a story.

"Story Illustrator" allows students to illustrate their work or simply to create a picture. Students can draw a picture themselves, use one from a "coloring book," or a combination of both. They can print their pictures, save them, or import them into stories.

"Story Player" is used by students to show off their stories. Illustrations are displayed with the stories and the students can hear their complete stories read to them. They may also print the complete stories.

"Icon Maker" allows students to create their own symbols for words. An icon is a small symbol or picture that can be used to represent something. *Kid Works 2* has some built-in icons; for example, the word *rain* can be represented by a small picture of raindrops. Figure 2.3 shows a story without icons and Figure 2.4 shows the same story with icons. Icons allow prereaders to write using the icons for difficult words. These small symbols/pictures are also another tool for creativity among students.

An example of a popular program that has been available for several years is *Dr. Peet's Talk/Writer* (Apple II series computers) by Dr. Peet (found in Edmark's catalog). This program motivates students by "singing" the letters of the alphabet as they are typed, allowing the students to make up their own ABC songs. This software uses very large letters, thus making it appropriate for prekindergarten and kindergarten students.

One component of this CAI package is a very simple word processor called "WriteWords." It allows students to write words, phrases, and short sentences. As a word is typed in, the computer will say the letters. When a student presses Return, the computer says the word, phrase, or short sentence.

Another option in *Dr. Peet's Talk/Writer* uses single-letters for file commands. For example, if a student wishes to save on disk the sentences he or she has written, the student uses the command **S** for save. There are only a few of these commands that the student must learn. In addition to the "S" command, *Dr. Peet's Talk/Writer* uses **R** for reading from disk, **Q** for quitting the program, **L** for loading from disk, and **P** for printing a file. These simple commands represent an excellent way for students to start learning about how computers operate. They cover most of the basic computer operations.

Another component of this CAI package teaches letter recognition. Letters appear in large print on the screen, and the package has a double-touch option where the first press of a letter key results in the letter being spoken, and the second press of the key results in the letter being written to the screen. Students delight in using this part of *Dr. Peet's Talk/Writer* to make up their own ABC songs.

Middle school and secondary students benefit by using a "professional" word-processing program that should transfer to the job setting after school. Word-processing skills also help in college. Two word-processing packages are

FIGURE 2.3 **Story without Icons**

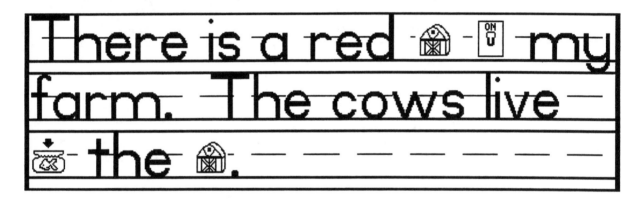

FIGURE 2.4 **Story with Icons**

used extensively in business: *WordPerfect* by WordPerfect Corporation (Macintosh, IBM, and IBM compatible computers) and *Microsoft Word* by Microsoft (Macintosh, IBM, and IBM compatible computers). Either of these is an excellent choice for secondary students. When teaching these word-processing packages, teachers should not try to teach the student the entire manual. Most people never need all the capabilities of the these two programs.

SAMS 10 Minute Guides (see Appendix II) are excellent manuals for the beginning student. These books teach the student the basics first and then a few of the fancy aspects of the word-processing packages. For example, if the student is using *WordPerfect*, then he or she would use *SAMS 10 Minute Guide to WordPerfect*. These books begin with starting the program, setting up the mouse, setting up the menus, and quitting the word-processing program. They then proceed to teach the student how to enter text, make menu selections, make editing changes, enhance text, and so on. These guides give clear step-by-step instructions and include pictures of the computer screens. They are excellent books for beginners because they assume no prior knowledge of the word-processing package. If you would like to look at one of these books, they can be found in most bookstores.

If a student is not ready for a professional word-processing package, he or she could use an intermediate package such as *The Bank Street Writer III* by Scholastic Software. However, the student should progress to *WordPerfect* or a similar professional program as soon as possible.

A few words need to be said about keyboard skills. The absence of keyboard skills is a significant problem for students in today's world. Hunt-and-peck students may become frustrated when working on long assignments, and the usefulness of computer mastery will be largely lost on students who do not have keyboard skills. However, there are numerous tutorials to teach keyboard skills to students at all levels. We highly recommend that this skill be developed in all students from the early elementary grades on. The more keyboard skills a student has, the more comfortable he or she will be with CAI. This topic is discussed in more detail in Chapter 4 along with using computers in the classroom and integration of CAI.

The activity in Try This 2.5 is designed to document how you currently use CAI software and in what ways you can expand your use of CAI software. If you just are starting to use computers in your classroom, you may wish to skip this activity and come back to it at a later time.

> ***Try This 2.5*** *Start a log of computer uses in your classroom. Your log should include the date, student, type of activity, grade, level of this activity, and CAI time. Form 2.5 is provided for this activity.*

Conclusion

In this chapter, we have discussed the characteristics of at-risk students and characteristics of CAI that may help these students. We then talked about instructional software consisting of initial instruction software, mastery practice software, and applications software, which included simulations and problem-solving CAI. We reviewed the advantages and disadvantages of each of these types of CAI. Using computers as tools in learning was also discussed.

The two activities in Try This 2.6 and 2.7 may be used as a guide to the sections of the next chapter that most interest you.

> ***Try This 2.6*** *List the ways you would like your students to use a computer in their curriculum. Form 2.6 can help with this activity. Keep this form for use with the next chapter.*

FORM 2.5
Computer Use Log

Date	Student	Type of Activity	Level of Activity	Grade	CAI Time

FORM 2.6

Goals for Computer Use in My Classroom

1. What types of mastery practice software would my students benefit from?

    _____

    _____

2. What simulation software could help my students?

    _____

    _____

3. Will I need to help my students learn how to play a "role" with simulation software?

    _____

    _____

4. What content material do I plan to introduce to my students using CAI?

    _____

    _____

5. Is there software that can help me introduce this new material?

    _____

    _____

6. What problem-solving skills could my students use help with?

    _____

    _____

***Try This* 2.7** *Describe the tasks for which you already use computers. Have the in-service director focus on what software is used or generate some ideas from this discussion concerning which software to review later on during the in-service.*

References

Boysen, T. C. (1994). Technology: An Educational Toolbox. *Technological Horizons in Education Journal*, 21(11), 10.

Caftori, N. (1994). Educational Effectiveness of Computer Software. *Technological Horizons in Education Journal*, 22(1), 62–65.

Daiute, C. (1986). Physical and Cognitive Factors in Revision: Insights from Studies with Computers. *Research in the Teaching of English*, 20, 141–159.

Horn, R., & Cleaves, A. (Eds.) (1980). *Guide to Simulations/Games for Education and Training*. Beverly Hills, CA.: Sage Publications.

Krasnor, L. R., & Mitterer, J. O. (1984). LOGO and the Development of General Problem-Solving Skills. *Alberta Journal of Educational Research*, 30(2), 133–144.

MacArthur, C. (1994). Peers + Word-Processing + Strategies = A Powerful Combination for Revising Student Writing. *Teaching Exceptional Children*, 27(1), 24–29.

Maddux, C. D., Johnson, D. L., & Willis, J. W. (1992). *Educational Computing: Learning with Tomorrow's Technologies*. Boston: MA. Allyn and Bacon.

Malouf, D. B., Jamison, P. J., Kercher, M. H., & Carlucci, C. M. (1991). Computer Software Aids Effective Instruction. *Teaching Exceptional Children*, 23(2), 56–57.

Malouf, D. B., Jamison, P. J., Kercher, M. H., & Carlucci, C. M. (1991). Integrating Computer Software into Effective Instruction. *Teaching Exceptional Children*, 23(3), 54–56.

Malouf, D. B., Jamison, P. J., Kercher, M. H., & Carlucci, C. M. (1991). Integrating Computer Software into Effective Instruction (Part 2). *Teaching Exceptional Children*, 23(4), 57–60.

Montague, M., & Fonseca, F. (1993). Using Computers to Improve Story Writing. *Teaching Exceptional Children*, 25(4), 46–60.

Sprinthall, N. A., & Sprinthall, R. C. (1990). *Educational Psychology* (5th ed.). New York, McGraw-Hill.

Vockell, E. L., & Mihail, T. (1993). Principles Behind Computerized Instruction for Students with Exceptionalities. *Teaching Exceptional Children*, 25(3), 39–43.

Willis, J., Hovey, L., & Hovey, K. (1987). *Computer Simulations: A Source Book to Learning in an Electronic Environment*. New York: Girlond Publishing.

3

Buying the Right Software

Renet L. Bender

*U*pon completion of this chapter you should be able to:

◆ *Prepare a list of your computer's attributes to purchase CAI software.*

◆ *Identify special hardware requirements of some CAI software.*

◆ *Perform applications evaluations of CAI software.*

◆ *Perform research evaluations of CAI software.*

Software selection is an acquired skill, and when master teachers learn this skill, their effective utilization of CAI software is greatly enhanced. The skills presented in this chapter will enable you to match CAI software to the needs of particular at-risk students in your class. When buying software for the classroom, teachers are typically given a software catalog with the titles of the software, a brief description, and price. Using this information, teachers are expected to choose software appropriate for their students. This system for software selection is clearly not optimal. However, even with the limited information available on this basis, teachers can make informed and appropriate software selections.

Evaluating software involves two skills. The most frequently discussed of these is the *applications evaluation*. In this type of evaluation, the teacher looks at attributes of the CAI software in relation to the characteristics of the children. For example, age appropriateness, skill level, types of reinforcement, and other factors are considered and a decision about use of the software is made. This discussion will include compatibility of software with computers and hardware, special hardware requirements, evaluations of software, locating software, and software support (i.e., what the software companies will do to help you choose the best software). In Chapter 2, we looked at several types of software for use in the classroom. As we discussed the different types of CAI, we introduced the ideas of pacing, errorless instruction, reinforcement, and feedback. These four concepts are important in the applications evaluation and selection of software for the classroom, and each is described here.

The second type of evaluation is the evaluation of the documented efficiency of the software for instructional purposes: the *research evaluation*. All professionals must keep up with the current research literature in their field—lawyers read law journals, doctors read medical journals, nurses read nursing journals, and so on. The master teacher is a professional, and therefore must keep up with the current literature in his or her specialty. In particular, if a teacher is going to use CAI software in the classroom, then he or she should look at what the current research literature says about CAI software. In the research literature, the master teacher will find the most recent methods for using CAI software to best benefit his or her students. Further, the research literature often contains information concerning the use of specific CAI packages. Master teachers should seek out information on the efficiency of a particular CAI package before utilization in the classroom.

It is crucial that master teachers not only learn to evaluate software but also to be able to utilize current research literature. When a teacher has mastered these two skills, he or she will be able to make better CAI selections for both the students and the budget, and to use CAI software in ways that will benefit at-risk students.

The Computer in Your Classroom

Only a few years ago, when purchasing software for a computer, all one had to know was if the computer in the classroom was an Apple, an IBM, or an IBM compatible computer. Today, when considering the purchase of software, this information is not adequate. For example, to run certain software, the computer must have a hard drive. Other software may require a large amount of memory (also known as random access memory, or RAM). Recently developed CAI packages often require a CD-ROM capability, discussed in Chapter 6. In this section, we will help you make a list of attributes for your computer. This list will aid you in using your computer more effectively and in purchasing software. If you are already quite familiar with your machine, you may wish to skip this section and start the section on Applications Evaluations.

Common Computers

The first thing you need to know is if your classroom computer is an Apple, an IBM, or an IBM compatible computer. IBM and IBM compatible machines are quite common in classrooms, but, by far, the most common computer in education is the Apple. Apple Computer has constructed two lines of computers that are commonly found in classrooms. Most public school classes started with Apple II series computers, including the Apple IIe, the Apple IIc, and the Apple IIGS. A second Apple computer line in education is the Macintosh series, which consists of the original Macintosh, the Macintosh LC, and the Power Macintosh computers. Among the Macintosh series, only the Macintosh LC will run software from the Apple IIe series computers (this is possible only if the computer has a particular internal component, an Apple IIe card, installed).

Operating System

The machine itself is not as important as the operating system and hardware components that comprise the machine. The operating system is the program that makes the computer usable; it is the program that is automatically run when the computer is switched on. If the computer is an Apple or a Macintosh, you should note the type of computer. If the computer is an IBM or an IBM compatible, you should know the name of the company that manufactured the machine and which operating system it uses; also note the version of the operating system.

If the computer is an IBM or an IBM compatible computer, you need to know if it has *Windows*. *Windows* is technically not an operating system but an applications program that works closely with the operating system to make the computer user friendly. If a computer uses *Windows*, there is no need to discover what operating system is used by the computer. However, the version of *Windows* needs to be identified. The version can be seen on the computer screen when the computer is turned on.

There are several ways to obtain information on the operating system. One method is to switch on the computer and look to see if the name and version of the operating system appear on the computer screen. Another is to look at the label on the diskette that is used to "boot" the computer system or check the label on the backup diskettes that came with the computer system. For example, some Leading Edge computers present the operating system (MS-DOS version 5.0) information when the computer is turned on, but Packard Bell computers do not, even though both are IBM-compatible computers.

Since the topic of operating systems and *Windows* is confusing to most people, we will summarize, in order, the questions that need to be asked about the computer.

1. What brand is your computer (Apple, Macintosh, IBM, Tandy, etc)?
2. If your computer is an Apple or Macintosh, what type is it (Apple IIe, Apple IIGS, Macintosh LC, Power Macintosh, etc.)?
3. If your computer is not an Apple or Macintosh, does it run *Windows*? If yes, what version?
4. If your computer is not an Apple or Macintosh and it does not run *Windows*, what operating system does it have? What version?

Diskettes

You need to know what type of diskettes are required for your computer. Diskettes come in two sizes. The larger diskettes are 5¼ inches and the smaller diskettes are 3½ inches. With either diskette size, you need to know if your computer uses HD (high density) or DD (double density) diskettes. DD diskettes were invented before HD diskettes; typically, machines that require DD diskettes cannot use HD diskettes. However, the machines that use HD diskettes can usually use the older DD diskettes also.

CD-ROM Drive

Many computers now have a CD-ROM drive. This disk drive usually looks similar to a compact disk player for music. Furthermore, the CD-ROM disks look like CDs that are used to play music. Newer versions of software are frequently sold on CD-ROM. The move from floppy disks to CD-ROM disks is occurring due to the fact that CD-ROM disks contain considerably more storage space than the conventional floppy disks. For example, the program *Kid Works 2* (discussed in Chapter 2) is available on CD-ROM. The CD-ROM with this software package contains the software version for *Windows* and the version for Macintosh. The buyer then installs the version appropriate for his or her computer.

When using CD-ROM disks, it should be noted that these disks are usually used only for storage. For example, in Chapter 6 we discuss multimedia. This type of software uses CD-ROM to store information such as pictures and text, but, unlike floppy disks, you never write to the CD-ROM disk. The technology behind these special disks is discussed in more detail in Chapter 6.

Memory Space

If there is a hard drive—an internal disk memory storage system—the amount of memory space available on the hard drive should be obtained. If the computer is an IBM or an IBM compatible that runs *Windows*, exit *Windows* and follow the instructions for a computer running DOS. If the computer is an IBM or an IBM compatible computer using DOS, this information can be easily obtained. Type in the command **DIR** at the DOS prompt (i.e., C:\>). At the end of the listing that appears on the computer screen, there will be the number of bytes free. A byte is the smallest amount of storage a program can access and one byte is composed of eight pieces of information; the smallest school computers typically include 64,000 bytes. Figure 3.1 shows

FIGURE 3.1 *Information Screen Showing Available Space*

OLDRIVE	<DIR>	09–10–92	12:33a
CODE	<DIR>	09–11–92	2:15a
LEWP	<DIR>	09–11–92	1:52a
HCD	<DIR>	09–11–92	2:18a
PCTEX	<DIR>	09–11–92	2:23a
QUE	<DIR>	09–11–92	2:43a
QAPLUS	<DIR>	09–11–92	2:43a
LB	<DIR>	09–11–92	2:44a
PACIOLI	<DIR>	09–11–92	2:44a
PAS	<DIR>	09–11–92	2:47a
TP	<DIR>	09–11–92	2:47a
GASPER	<DIR>	09–11–92	2:52a
LOTUS	<DIR>	09–11–92	2:52a
MANAGER	<DIR>	09–11–92	2:54a
BASIC	<DIR>	09–11–92	2:54a
PFS	<DIR>	09–11–92	2:55a
MSWORKS	<DIR>	10–02–92	8:42a
DBSAMPLE	<DIR>	10–22–92	9:49p
VIRUS	<DIR>	11–28–92	3:33p
TC	<DIR>	01–25–93	10:17a
GA	<DIR>	05–27–93	11:23a

	33 files(s)	49139 bytes
		6166528 bytes free

an example of this information from an IBM compatible computer. At the end of the listing, it says that the hard drive has 6166528 bytes free; in other words, 6 megabytes are available (1 megabyte is 1 million bytes). If you wish to get back to *Windows*, type **win** at the prompt and press Enter.

If the computer is an Apple or Macintosh with a hard drive, pull down the menu under file. Click the mouse on "get info" or something similar to one of the following: "disk top," "hard disk," or "system." A window will appear on the screen containing information. One of the lines should give the number of bytes or kilobytes free. One kilobyte (K) is equal to 1,000 bytes.

RAM Memory

Another item of importance is the amount of available RAM (random access memory) on the computer. This information can usually be found in the manuals associated with the computer. If the computer has *Windows*, exit and follow the instructions for a computer running DOS. If the computer is an IBM or an IBM compatible computer using DOS operating system, type the command **MEM** at the prompt "C:\>." The amount of RAM on the computer will appear on the screen. Figure 3.2 shows an example of this. The important information is the "largest executable program size." As seen in Figure 3.2, this computer has 580,240 bytes, or 580K of RAM, available.

If the computer is an Apple or Macintosh, pull down the menu under the apple. Click on one of the following: "about the finder," "disk top," "system," or "memory." One of these choices should divulge the amount of RAM on the computer system. If using other Apple computers, the exact amount of RAM they contain can be found in the manual for that computer. Typically, the Apple IIe and IIc have 64K (i.e., 64 kilobytes) and the Apple IIGS has between 256K and 516K.

Monitor

Finally, you will need to know if your monitor is a color monitor or a monochrome monitor. If the computer is an IBM or an IBM compatible computer, you will probably need an IBM color graphics card to run most software. Other names for an IBM color graphics card are VGA graphics and EGA graphics. EGA graphics is an older version, and machines that have EGA graphics cannot typically be used with software that requires VGA graphics. However, software that requires EGA graphics will run using VGA graphics.

> ***Try This 3.1*** *Switch on the computer and answer the questions on Form 3.1.*

FIGURE 3.2   Available RAM

C: \ >mem

655360	bytes total conventional memory
655360	bytes available to MS-DOS
580240	largest executable program size
262144	bytes total contiguous extended memory
262144	bytes available contiguous extended memory

FORM 3.1

Getting to Know My Computer

1. What type of computer am I using?

2. If my computer is an IBM or IBM compatible computer, does it have Windows? _____
   If yes, what version? _____

3. If my computer is an IBM or IBM compatible that does not have Windows, what operating system does it have? _____

4. Does my computer have a hard drive? _____

5. How much space is available on it? _____

6. What size diskettes do my floppy drives use? _____

7. Can they be double density or high density? _____

8. Does my computer have a CD-ROM drive? _____

9. How much RAM is available? _____

10. Is my monitor a color monitor or a monochrome monitor? _____

Once the list in Form 3.1 is complete, keep it in a convenient place for easy reference. Most software companies provide the prospective buyer with easy-to-read software compatibility charts. These charts are usually located at the back of their catalogs. Other companies put the hardware requirements as footnotes at the bottom of the page in their catalogs. Addresses for several software companies may be found in Appendix II.

Special Hardware Requirements

In this section, we will briefly describe the most common peripheral requirements of software for at-risk students. These peripherals include speech synthesizers, touch screens, the mouse, Apple IIe emulation cards, Muppet Learning Keys, Intellikeys, and others. Furthermore, we will give an idea of what these peripherals are, approximately how much they cost, and enough information to decide if you can personally install the peripheral yourself.

Speech Synthesizer

A substantial portion of newer software for at-risk students uses the Echo speech synthesizer produced by Echo Speech Corporation (These can be ordered through Edmark, listed at the end of the book in Appendix II). This device allows the computer to "talk" to students. The Echo speech synthesizer has several versions depending on the type of computer. For example, the Echo II is for the Apple IIe and Apple IIGS computers, and the Echo LC is for Apple IIc/IIc+ computers and the Macintosh LC when running in Apple IIe emulation mode. The Echo PC II is for IBM and IBM compatible computers, and the Echo PC is for all computers.

Both the Echo LC and the Echo PC are stand-alone devices. This means that you simply plug them into a particular port on the computer. The Echo II and the Echo PC II consist of boards that are installed inside the computer. Obviously the stand-alone versions are easier to install, but with good instructions teachers have installed both types. In either case, there will also be an external speaker and a jack for headphones. The price of a speech synthesizer is typically between $100 and $200.

Touch Screen

Another peripheral that is widely used, especially with younger and at-risk students, is the touch screen. This special screen fits over the monitor screen. It allows the student to select his or her answer by touching the screen. This is an important device for students with extremely poor fine motor skills who may have difficulty typing their answers on the keyboard. The touch screen allows these students to use the computer like other students, which can improve their self-confidence. Moreover, the touch screen can be used as a beginning step in teaching students keyboard skills. This option is discussed in more detail in Chapter 4.

The touch screen easily attaches to the monitor with velcro strips. Prices for a touch screen vary from $300 to $400. These devices are typically installed by the teacher.

The Mouse

A mouse is a device that allows a person to communicate with the computer without using the keyboard. By moving the mouse on a flat surface next to the computer, a student can position the cursor on the monitor. Choices are indicated by pressing a button on the mouse. Today, a mouse is considered standard on many systems, but it may not have been a part of older systems. A mouse can easily be added to either a Macintosh or an IBM compatible computer by plugging the mouse into the serial port and running the installation software. The price for a mouse is usually around $50.

Apple IIe Emulation Card

When schools replaced their Apple IIe computers with Macintosh LC computers, they did not have to buy all new software. Apple makes a card that can be installed in Macintosh LC computers so that the Macintosh can run Apple IIe software. In other words, the Macintosh will act like or emulate an Apple IIe when this card is installed. This emulation card is only made for the Macintosh LC and can be installed by teachers by following the directions. They range in price from $100 to $200.

Muppet Learning Keys

Muppet Learning Keys (by WINGS for Learning/Sunburst Communications) is an alternative keyboard; it arranges the keys in alphabetical order. No additional hardware is required to install this peripheral, but it can be used only with software that is written specifically for it. Muppet Learning Keys costs around $200 and is available for Macintosh, Apple, and IBM PS/2 computers.

IntelliKeys

IntelliKeys, by IntelliTools, is another alternative keyboard that allows modification for students. It was designed for young students and students with disabilities. The keyboard is basically a plastic membrane, and the teacher has a choice of six overlays. Overlays are plastic covers that are placed over the membrane and dictate what locations on the membrane do what functions. Figure 3.3 is an example of the overlay for the alphabet giving the student large keys. Custom overlays can be designed for specialized applications.

By sliding an overlay into the IntelliKeys keyboard, the teacher tells the device which setup to use. The keys on each overlay are specially designed to be large enough for students with physical disabilities and easily comprehended by students with learning disabilities. Furthermore, IntelliKeys has features that allow the teacher to adjust the responsiveness of the keyboard. For example, one adjustment allows the teacher to determine if multiple repeated letters appear when a key is held down. IntelliKeys, with its large keys and colorful overlays, appeals to all students, not just students with disabilities.

IntelliKeys is plugged into the keyboard port of the computer and is available for Apple IIe computers with an IntelliKeys IIe card, Apple IIGS computers, and most Macintosh, IBM, and IBM compatible computers. Teachers can use IntelliKeys with any software, which is a distinct advantage over Muppet Keys (discussed earlier). IntelliKeys ranges in price from $350 to $450.

FIGURE 3.3 *Plastic Overlay*

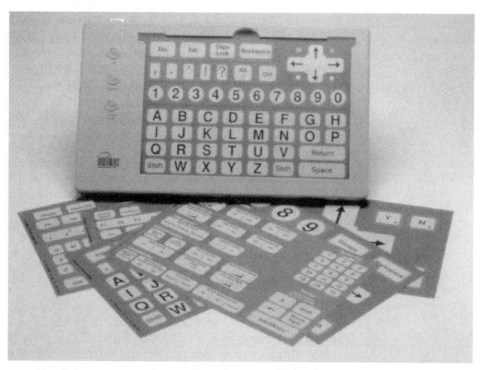

Summary

In summary, speech synthesizers, touch screens, a mouse, Apple IIe emulation cards, Muppet Learning Keys, and IntelliKeys are common peripherals. Most of these peripherals may be found in computer stores and in some software catalogs such as Edmark's catalog. Other equipment can be found by calling the manufacturer. Information on these companies can be found in Appendix II.

Applications Evaluations

Attributes of the CAI Software

Choosing the right software for at-risk students is not difficult when using a list of CAI software attributes to help in the evaluation of software. There are numerous forms elaborating on software attributes to assist you in the selection of CAI software (Maddux, Johnson, & Willis 1992; Lewis 1993; Bitter, Camuse, & Durbin 1993). In Chapter 2, we discussed five types of CAI software—namely, initial instruction, mastery practice, simulations, problem-solving, and word-processing software. When evaluating CAI software for use in the classroom, there are software attributes that should be considered regardless of the type. There are also software attributes that should be considered when evaluating a particular type of CAI software. Each of these will be discussed in this chapter. Appendix II contains a list of software sources.

Initial Questions

Before looking at a piece of software, teachers should consider several questions. What is the content area in which you are interested in using CAI? What are the academic levels of the students included in this lesson? What is the intended use of the software? What are the learning objectives of the lesson(s) for which the software may be used? Armed with such information, you are now ready to locate software and evaluations.

The activity in Try This 3.2 is intended to guide you through the important questions that should be asked when choosing software. If you are already familiar with software selection, you may wish to skip this activity.

> ***Try This 3.2*** *Choose a lesson with which you would like to use CAI. Answer the important questions for that lesson on Form 3.2. List your students who will use this lesson and their learning characteristics, as described in Chapter 2.*

FORM 3.2
Preevaluation for Software Needs

1. What is the content area of the lesson?_____
   _____

2. What is the intended use of the CAI software?_____
   _____
   _____

3. List the objectives for the lesson(s). _____
   _____
   _____

4. Which software category (or categories) would best suit your intended use and learning
   objectives? _____
   _____

5. What is the rough academic skill level of your students for which this lesson(s) is intended? _____
   _____

6. What are the ages of the students for which this lesson(s) is intended? _____
   _____

7. List students who will use this lesson(s) and their learning characteristics.

Students	**Characteristics**
a. _____	_____
	_____
	_____
b. _____	_____
	_____
	_____
c. _____	_____
	_____
	_____
d. _____	_____
	_____
	_____

Applications Evaluations

After identifying your needs, the next step is to locate software and evaluations of the software. There are two kinds of applications evaluations to help in the selection of CAI software: internal and external evaluations.

External evaluations are those done by organizations outside the school system. For example, these would include evaluations done by software companies, computer companies, magazines or journals, and professional organizations. When using external evaluations, there are two considerations of which teachers should be cognizant (Maddux, Johnson, & Willis, 1992).

1. The evaluation may be biased. For example, if a software company has invested a large sum of money into the development of a particular program, it will naturally present the software as an excellent program. If a program was written for a certain brand of computer, that computer company may use the software as a selling point for its computers and therefore will present the software in a good light.
2. The evaluation may not have been done by a qualified person. When an evaluation done by a professional organization appears in a magazine or journal, it is not known if the evaluation was performed by someone who is familiar with the needs of at-risk students. It is common for some evaluators to prepare an evaluation based on their own teaching experience without particular consideration for at-risk students. Also, the evaluator's teaching experience may be limited to a certain grade level. For example, the evaluator could have experience with five-year-olds and the software could be intended for use with secondary students.

With these two points in mind, teachers may wonder why they should look at external evaluations. Of course, the best type of evaluation is the internal, or hands-on, evaluation. However, external evaluations can be used cautiously to help in initial screening of CAI software. External evaluations can help teachers decide if the software may be appropriate for their students. Because no master teacher has excess time to evaluate a lot of software, external evaluations can be used to help a teacher identify the type of CAI software he or she wishes to use.

Figure 3.4 contains a list of sources for external software evaluations. In addition to these sources, there are several other ways to find out about external software evaluations. One easy way is to ask other teachers what CAI software they use and see if they have read evaluations. Also, ask their opinion of the software. Another source of good information is conference participants. Talk to other participants attending professional conferences devoted to CAI and technology, and ask them about their recommendations. Check to see if software companies have exhibits that include displays of software at conferences. Other sources of information on CAI software include magazines and journals, some of which are listed at the end of the chapter and in Figure 3.5. Also, several software companies are listed in Appendix II.

The second kind of applications evaluation is the *internal evaluation*, which is completed by you or people in your organization. For example, an internal evaluation may have already been done by another teacher in the school, a teacher in the county, or a computer specialist working with the school system.

FIGURE 3.4 *Sources for External Software Evaluations*

Special Needs Software Guide Apple Foundation 20525 Mariani Avenue Cupertino, CA 95014	Closing the Gap P.O. Box 68 Henderson, MN 56044
Center for Special Education Information Exchange The Council for Exceptional Children 1920 Association Drive Reston, VA 22091	Educational Software Exchange Library (EDSEL) c/o Stanford Avenue School 2833 Illinois Avenue Southgate, CA 90281
EPIE Institute Teachers' College Columbia University 525 W. 120th Street New York, NY 10027	International Council for Computers in Education University of Oregon Eugene, OR 97403
LINC Resources Inc. 3857 N. High Street Columbus, OH 43214	Microcomputer Information Coordination 139 C.R.U. K.U.M.C. 9th and Rainbow Kansas City, KS 66103
MicroSIFT Project Northwest Regional Educational Laboratory 710 S.W. 2nd Avenue Portland, OR 97204	National Education Association Educational Computer Service 4720 Montgomery Lane Bethesda, MD 20814
Software Reports 10996 Torreyana Road P.O. Box 85007 San Diego, CA 92138	Special Education Software Review 3807 N. Northwood Peoria, IL 61614

FIGURE 3.5 *Journals and Magazines*

Technological Horizons in Education Journal 150 El Camino Real Suite 112 Tustin, CA 92680–3670	Intervention in School and Clinic Pro-ED 8700 Shoal Creek Blvd. Austin, TX 78757–6897
Exceptional Children Council for Exceptional Children 1920 Association Drive Reston, VA 22091	Teaching Exceptional Children 1920 Association Drive Reston, VA 22091–1589

To reiterate, the best kind of evaluation is hands-on, which allows you, the teacher, to get a true feel for the software. When teachers are beginning the search for CAI software, they should take advantage of software fairs, vendor demonstrations, demonstration classrooms, and educational computer conferences. Software companies will be pleased to let teachers try out their software at these events. Teachers can sit down with a representative from the company and work through the software while asking questions. Teachers can also get literature containing information on the software to take back to their schools. Furthermore, teachers are sometimes allowed to take a demonstration disk with which to do an extensive internal evaluation. These events are highly recommended by teachers for discovering CAI software. In some cases, participants of these events may be eligible for discounts on the software displayed.

Before a teacher personally evaluates software selections extensively, he or she should check to see if there are internal evaluations of the software at a central location in his or her school or school district. Next, the teacher should check with other teachers. Finally, if an internal evaluation of the software has not been found, the teacher should do one.

As mentioned earlier, there are numerous forms available to help teachers with internal applications evaluations. Some of these forms are to be used with all types of CAI software (Lewis, 1993; Maddux, Johnson, & Willis, 1992) and some forms are to be used for particular types of CAI software (Bitter, Camuse, & Durbin, 1993). We chose to use one form with different sections for particular types of CAI software. You can modify this form for your individual needs.

Try This 3.3 *The form we recommend for software evaluation is presented in Form 3.3. Follow along with this form while we discuss the particular concerns covered in it.*

FORM 3.3
CAI Software Applications Evaluation

SUBJECT

Area: _____

Topic(s): _____

Program Name: _____

Publisher: _____

Address: _____

Telephone: _____

Price: _____

Brief Description of Software: _____

_____

_____

_____

_____

_____

_____

_____

Rate the remaining topics between 0 and 5, with 0 indicating poor and 5 excellent.

Content	**Rating**
1. Accurate content	_____
2. Accomplishes stated objectives	_____
3. Age appropriate	_____
4. Skill level appropriate	_____
TOTAL FOR CONTENT	_____

Presentation	**Rating**
1. Program bug free	_____
2. Clear instructions	_____
3. Appropriate reinforcement	_____
4. Appropriate use of color and graphics	_____
5. Appropriate use of sound	_____
6. Variable pacing	_____

7. Appropriate sequencing   _____

8. Readability of text appropriate for user   _____

   TOTAL FOR PRESENTATION   _____

Teacher Use	**Rating**

1. Keeps useful performance records   _____

2. Curriculum objectives stated clearly   _____

3. Suggestions for integration into curriculum   _____

4. No need for instructor assistance   _____

5. Interesting follow-up activities or
   projects suggested   _____

6. Teacher manual is useful   _____

7. Prerequisite student skills clearly stated   _____

8. Adequate documentation   _____

   TOTAL FOR TEACHER USE   _____

User Friendliness	**Rating**

1. Instructions are reviewable at any time   _____

2. Students can exit the program at any time   _____

3. Students can restart program where they stopped   _____

4. Allows correction of typing errors   _____

5. Incorrect selection of keys does not cause
   the program to crash   _____

6. Clear summary of program operations provided   _____

7. Requires no computer knowledge   _____

8. High student involvement   _____

   TOTAL FOR USER FRIENDLINESS   _____

INITIAL INSTRUCTION AND MASTERY PRACTICE

Attributes	**Rating**

1. Provides students with performance record   _____

2. Student controls rate of presentation   _____

3. Student controls sequence of lesson   _____

4. Student controls selection of lesson   _____

5. Student can choose style of presentation   _____

6. Can review previous screens of information   _____

7. Errorless learning feature   _____

8. Does not require student to manipulate disk drive   _____

9. Random generation of problems   _____

TOTAL FOR INITIAL INSTRUCTION
AND MASTERY PRACTICE ATTRIBUTES   _____

SIMULATION

Attributes	**Rating**
1. Realistic simulation of events	_____
2. Students do not need to refer to reference manuals	_____
3. High student involvement	_____
4. Encourages cooperation	_____
5. Time of simulation is appropriate	_____
TOTAL FOR SIMULATION ATTRIBUTES	_____

PROBLEM SOLVING

Attributes	**Rating**
1. Skills required of student are clearly stated	_____
2. Skills the program enhances are stated	_____
3. Beginning skill level explains the basic steps for problem solving	_____
4. Skills helped by the program can transfer to other content areas	_____
5. Problems are randomly generated	_____
6. Reviews the problem or the basic steps to problem solving when a student misses a problem	_____
TOTAL FOR PROBLEM-SOLVING ATTRIBUTES	_____

WORD PROCESSING

Attributes	**Rating**
1. Documentation provides index and table of contents	_____
2. Clear, nicely formatted screen displays	_____
3. Incorrect selection of commands does not make the program crash	_____
4. Menus and help features make the program user friendly	_____

  5. Clear and useful summary of commands provided   _____

  6. Accepts abbreviations for common responses   _____

  7. Operation of program does not require student
     to turn the computer on and off   _____

  8. Commands easy to learn   _____

  9. Allows easy deleting, moving, and underlining
     of text   _____

10. Has word wrap feature   _____

11. Protective features to avoid loss of files   _____

12. Entire width of text can be seen on the monitor   _____

13. Loading, saving, and printing files is easy   _____

14. Use of word-processing program does not require
     intermittent access to master disk   _____

     TOTAL FOR WORD-PROCESSING ATTRIBUTES   _____

TOTAL POINTS   _____

RECOMMENDATION FOR THIS SOFTWARE:

Common Attributes of CAI Software

Content and Type of CAI

The content of a CAI software package may seem a bit obvious, but consider two packages we mentioned in the previous chapter: *Call the Parrot* and *Glowy*. Looking solely at the names of the software, teachers have no idea what the content is of these two packages. In fact, *Call the Parrot* teaches students the directions of north, south, east and west; and *Glowy* teaches students critical thinking skills for addition, subtraction, and whole-number concepts. It takes more knowledge than merely the name and "reading the wrapper" to effectively understand software.

When considering the content area of a CAI package, you should consider the objectives of the software. Do the stated objectives match the objectives of the curriculum plan for your students? If not, can the CAI objectives be modified to meet your objectives? Is the content material accurate? Questions such as these help you plan for more effective use of the CAI program.

CAI software is screened initially by content area and type. Note that a CAI program can be classified as more than one type. One example is *Words and Concepts* (discussed in Chapter 2). This software package can be used as an initial instruction program to introduce vocabulary words. It can also be used as a mastery practice program after the vocabulary words have been introduced. Simulations may also be classified as both problem-solving software and as initial instruction software. Form 3.3 is a software evaluation form discussed in this chapter. You should follow along on this form as each area of the applications evaluation is discussed. Also, you may wish to make copies of this form to use with all types of CAI software.

Age Appropriateness and Skill Level of CAI Software

Other important aspects of CAI software include age appropriateness (Gardner, Taber-Brown, & Wissick, 1992) and skill level. Suppose a teacher wants to drill a 13-year-old on vocabulary. If this student has the skill level of a student in second grade, the teacher would not drill him or her on software with a skill level at fifth grade. Furthermore, the teacher should be cognizant of how the material is presented. Software that drills a student using nursery rhymes will not appeal to a 13-year-old at-risk student.

Presentation of Material

In order to use CAI effectively, the software should help keep the student on task. This may involve several factors, some of which relate to the presentation methods chosen. Among these factors are graphics and auditory systems. Most effective CAI software uses a combination of these methods. Other aspects of presentation include how the program handles correct and incorrect answers from the student, pacing, and sequencing. There are several questions regarding the presentation that a teacher should ask:

1. *Is the program free of bugs?* A program is said to have a "bug" if it has an error in the program. Some bugs can be harmless and go unnoticed. An example of this is if the documentation tells the student to press Return to enter an answer, and, by trial and error, the student discovers he must press Return twice to enter the answer. At the other extreme, a bug in a program can cause it to "crash" (i.e., the computer will stop performance in the

middle of the program). For example, if the program crashes when the **ESC** key is pressed, the program has a major bug.

2. *Do the directions make clear what type of response is expected?* There is nothing more frustrating to a teacher or students than responding to the questions in the program in the appropriate manner and having the program say that an error was made. Another problem is when a teacher or student is responding appropriately to a question and the program does something unexpected that is not mentioned in the documentation.

3. *What happens when a wrong answer is given?* When a wrong answer is given, it is more helpful to the student if the program helps the student to discover what is wrong with his or her answer than for the program to ask the student to repeat the missed question. A program that just tells the student to "try again" is not very helpful in instructing the student and may result in a teacher spending more time monitoring students using that particular CAI program.

4. *What happens if several wrong answers are given?* When the student is consistently giving wrong answers, the program should either review the content material or tell the student to summon the teacher. Also, the program's response is related to the type of CAI package. For example, you should expect an initial instruction program to review the content material, whereas a mastery practice program would instruct the student to summon the teacher.

5. *Does the software do anything that is distracting to students?* With at-risk students, care should be taken in choosing software that does not distract them. Most of these students are easily distracted and find it difficult to stay on task. A loud noise or extremely flashy graphics can break a student's concentration. Therefore, both of these items should be avoided with certain at-risk students who may be easily distracted. A teacher may wish to try these programs once or twice with a particular student to determine if the program overly excites him or her.

6. *Is the CAI software self-paced or can the teacher vary the pacing?* As discussed in Chapter 2, pacing is the rate at which new material is introduced (i.e., the amount of time the student is given to answer questions). Programs can have automatic pacing or pacing can be determined by the teacher. The most flexible CAI programs will have both. For example the CAI package *Alligator Mix* (discussed in Appendix I) contains both types of pacing. *Alligator Mix* helps students increase their skill in addition and subtraction of numbers 0 through 9 by feeding alligators in a swamp. As alligators appear in the swamp, apples with addition and subtraction problems move toward the alligator's mouth. Answers appear in the stomach of the alligator. As the apples approach the alligator, the student must determine if the answer in the alligator is the correct answer for the approaching problem. If it is, the student must open the alligator's mouth by pressing a designated key allowing the alligator to eat the apple. The teacher has the option of setting the internal pacing level, which is the speed that the apples approach the alligator. After the student gets a certain number of correct answers, the program will automatically pick up the pace by increasing the speed of the apples and increasing the number alligators.

7. *Does the student have control over the sequencing?* Sequencing represents the order of presentation of the material. In other words, when a stu-

dent is working on a lesson, some CAI programs allow the student to choose particular exercises within the lesson, according to the student's individual curiosity. This variation is quite common in multimedia programs (discussed in Chapter 6). If a teacher uses CAI software that has student-controlled sequencing together with performance summaries, the teacher will find that students will usually make wise decisions concerning the exercises they need to work on, and therefore that teacher will spend less time monitoring students.

8. *The student should have the option of reviewing the directions at the beginning of the lesson or at any point during the lesson.*   An example of this is seen in *Math Shop Jr.,* in the program called "Flower Shop" (which is discussed in Appendix I). In this shop, customers come in and ask for a certain number of flowers. It is the student's job to choose one number from each of two given lists so that they equal the number of flowers the customer desires. When the student makes a mistake in filling the customer's order, the program informs the student of his or her error and repeats the directions for that game. This is particularly important for students who have difficulty with short- or long-term memory, and for students with attention problems.

Method of Instruction

The method of instruction includes feedback, reinforcement, and the range of ability the program accommodates (Vockell & Mihail, 1993). All of these are important in that their proper use will prevent students from becoming frustrated and anxious.

CAI programs should always give students immediate feedback. If a student answers correctly, the software should tell the student that he or she answered the question correctly and provide other reinforcement as necessary. Also, if a student answers a question incorrectly, the software should tell him or her to try again, to review the material, or to summon the teacher. Immediate feedback is one of the main reasons for using CAI software, as opposed to pencil and paper worksheets. Immediate feedback can motivate students when they are answering questions correctly and it can prevent students from getting wrong ideas if they are answering questions incorrectly.

Reinforcement is a type of feedback, but it should be more than that. For example, consider the two CAI software packages described here. The first package says "Good job!" every time a correct answer is given and "Try again" every time a question is answered incorrectly. The second package gives one of six congratulatory messages upon answering a question correctly, and after answering four consecutive questions correctly it displays colorful fireworks going off on the screen. After a question is answered incorrectly, this software package gives one of three messages that in effect tell the student that the answer was wrong and to try again. Furthermore, after a question is missed three times the CAI instructs the student to summon the teacher.

Most individuals would prefer the second CAI package. It behaves more like people expect a teacher to act. Furthermore, if the responses of the software become predictable, the reinforcement will lose potency and the students will not like to use that particular software.

In addition, the amount of reinforcement offered is a crucial concept. If a program offers reinforcement too frequently for a particular student, the reinforcement looses its value. If a program offers too little, the student's interest in the lesson will decrease. A CAI program should offer just enough reinforcement to motivate each student to continue. For this reason, effective

CAI packages will allow a teacher to vary the reinforcement level from one student to the next.

Some software will show very interesting graphics with sound effects when a student makes a mistake or a series of mistakes. In this case, the student quickly learns that it is more fun to respond with incorrect answers than with correct answers. Thus, CAI programs may reinforce the wrong ideas. This problem rarely occurs but should be considered.

Management of Student Performance

Computer management and assessment of students is discussed in Chapter 5. However, when evaluating a CAI package a few items should be noted. Does the software automatically keep student performance records? Is every student answer stored, such that a teacher can recheck the student's work and do an error analysis on a problem-by-problem basis? Is the stored information useful? Are the records stored on disk? Is the information useful and complete? Are the records secure? These questions are important when monitoring student performance, and should be included in any applications evaluation.

Documentation

Good documentation is necessary for effective use of any CAI package. Documentation is where a teacher will turn to find instructions on installation and running of the CAI software. The hardware requirements, discussed earlier, will be delineated here, as will the goals and objectives, prerequisite skills, and skill levels of the software. Furthermore, most documentation for CAI software will include suggestions for use in the classroom, student worksheets, and lesson plans. The documentation should also specify how to set up student records and modify pacing and reinforcement. Clearly, the documentation is an important aspect of CAI software. Good documentation will aid a teacher in setting up the software in a minimal amount of time, whereas inadequate documentation can lead to frustration and wasted time.

User Friendliness

User friendliness is a term that most people have heard. We will look at what user friendliness means with respect to CAI software and students. Think about the ideal CAI software. The student should be able to use it with minimal teacher interaction. The software should have clear, on-screen directions. The student should be able to exit the program at any time, restarting the program later at exactly the same place in the program. An interesting example of this is the simulation software *Oregon Trail*. The version that was discussed in Chapter 2, is the version for the Macintosh. In this version, the student is able to stop the simulation and exit at anytime. Furthermore, the student can restart the program where he or she stopped previously. This is not true for the older Apple IIe version of that software. The result is that students are always starting over and they never reach Oregon using the older version. This feature is important, particularly with simulation software, since this type of software is usually used over several class periods or lessons.

There are a few other things that can cause difficulties with students and that should be checked, such as:

1. Does the program allow correction of typing errors?
2. Are loading and running instructions clear?
3. Does incorrect selection of keys cause the program to stop running?

All of these problems are common to many types of CAI software. If a program is poorly designed in any of these areas, it can result in more of the teacher's time monitoring students, leaving both teachers and students feeling frustrated, anxious, and reluctant to use CAI.

The activity in Try This 3.4 is designed to guide you through your first software evaluation. If you have previously done extensive software evaluations, you may which to skip this activity.

> **Try This 3.4**   *Use Form 3.3 to evaluate a CAI program for the attributes described in this section. These attributes are included in the first two pages of the form.*

Type-Specific Characteristics of CAI Software

Earlier, we discussed characteristics that are common to all types of CAI software. We will now focus on attributes that are more specific to particular types of software. You can follow along on the remaining pages of Form 3.3.

Initial Instruction and Mastery Practice

Initial instruction and mastery practice use traditional techniques for teaching students during the initial instruction and practice phases of learning. When evaluating these two types of CAI software, a teacher should also give consideration to the following attributes.

After a practice session, students should be provided with information about their performance. This information can motivate the students and let them know in which areas they need to work. Perhaps the teacher could chart the students' correct answers daily and provide extra reinforcement when the number of correct answers increases. This is a very effective instructional technique because youngsters love to see charts of their own performance increases.

Students should be allowed to read new information and directions for the program at their own rate. Most CAI programs accomplish this by asking students to press a key after they have read the screen of information. This prevents students from getting frustrated and anxious about how to use the program. If the pacing is controllable, the teacher may allow individual students to go at their own speed until their competence improves and then increase the pace.

In some cases, it is appropriate to allow students to choose particular exercises in a lesson, a particular lesson, or the style of presentation. For example, some students may prefer lessons with a game-like format similar to a maze, while others may prefer puzzle-like formats. Effective CAI offers both.

Students should be able to review previous screens of information. For instance, *Rocky's Boots* by the Learning Company is a program that teaches students general problem-solving skills. The goal of the program is for the student to use given components to built machines that solve certain problems. For the student to attain the ability to build machines, there are skills and rules that he or she must learn. *Rocky's Boots* is structured so that at any time the student can review previous information concerning the skills and rules of building machines.

A potential problem with any CAI software is intermittent operation of a single disk drive. For example, when using the older version of the CAI software package *Math Blaster Mystery* (discussed in Chapter 2) for the Apple IIe, the student is repeatedly asked to turn the disk over. Most modern software does not have this requirement, but the teacher should show care in avoiding this type of problem.

Errorless learning procedures, discussed in Chapter 2, are an excellent feature for initial instruction and mastery practice CAI software. It can be extremely difficult for at-risk students to learn new material or to attain competence in certain material, whereas the errorless learning procedures can help students learn new material or practice on material without becoming frustrated. The procedures discussed in *Words and Concepts* help the students to attain 90 percent accuracy quickly. The teacher can then move individual students to the next level, where the errorless feature is put to use only if a student misses a question.

If you do not have any initial instruction or mastery practice software, you may wish to skip the activity given in Try This 3.5.

> ***Try This 3.5*** *Choose an initial instruction or mastery practice program and answer the questions provided in the initial instruction and master practice section of Form 3.3. Which of these characteristics are important to you and your students? Are there other characteristics you can think of?*

Simulations

Evaluation of simulations was discussed briefly in Chapter 2. We will now examine in greater depth the attributes of simulations that should be considered when evaluating them.

Realistic simulation of events is an important characteristic to notice. Most simulations are similar to real life but vary in the details. For example, on the real Oregon Trail, the settlers also had to contend with Indians and outlaws, but these are not mentioned in the simulation. As a master teacher, you should take notes on how the simulation program differs from real life and discuss these differences with students after the simulation is over. The students may be able to point out a few other places where the simulation and real life differ, which is a very effective, postsimulation learning activity for at-risk students.

Simulation activities can be very complex for at-risk students to learn. Teachers should check the available references in the school library and provide reference material to the students as they work with the simulation. Films and videos may be used before simulations to introduce the problems encountered later. Many teachers find that students who are usually reluctant to use an encyclopedia for ordinary school reports will utilize these references much more frequently to support a CAI simulation activity.

Another characteristic of simulations is that they call for high student involvement. Simulations are flexible in that one student, a group of students, or the entire class can participate. You should also consider how well the program encourages cooperation between at-risk students and others.

Finally, the time requirement of the simulation should be noted. Most simulations require longer than a class period to use. Find out if the CAI simulation can be broken down into class lessons easily. Try the activity in Try This 3.6.

> ***Try This 3.6*** *Choose a simulation package and answer the questions in the simulation section in Form 3.3. Are there any characteristics of simulations that are important to you and your students that you can add?*

Problem Solving

As we saw earlier in Chapter 2, problem-solving software can be subject specific and nonsubject specific. When using this type of software, a teacher should be careful to note the skills required of the students. It can be frustrating to students to have problems forced on them before they have adequate skills.

One attribute of problem-solving software that should be considered is whether the beginning skill level in the CAI program takes the student through the basic problem-solving steps. An example of this attribute was discussed in Chapter 2. As seen in *Math Blaster Mystery,* "Follow the Steps," showing students the basic steps in problem solving can be helpful.

A teacher should note the problem-solving skills that the software is designed to help the student with. Are these general skills or subject-specific skills? Can these skills be used in other areas? If a teacher wants these skills to generalize to other areas, he or she should discuss generalization with the students. Start by asking, In what other situations could you use these skills?

With subject-specific problem-solving software, there is usually a given set of problems for the student to solve. A teacher should ask several questions about the presentation of these problems. Are the problems generated randomly? In other words, does the information change in the problems and are the problems presented in a different order every time the program is used? After using the program a few times, have the students memorized the problems and their order? A teacher will, of course, want to avoid any problem-solving software that allows students to memorize the problems and their solutions.

What happens when the student misses a problem? Does the software review the information in the problem? Does the software help the student through the basic steps of problem solving? Does the software just repeat the problem until the student gets it right? If problem-solving software repeats a problem that the student just missed, and if the student misses the problem a second time, the software should instruct the student to summon the teacher. Refer to the activity in Try This 3.7.

Try This 3.7   *Choose a problem-solving program and answer the questions in the problem-solving section of Form 3.3.*

Word Processing

The attributes to be evaluated in a word-processing package concern the operation of the program and the documentation. When evaluating these attributes, a teacher should always bear in mind the abilities of his or her students.

First, the documentation should be complete. It should provide an index and a table of contents and full instructions on utilization. The information concerning the installation and running of the program should be written in clear steps that are easy to follow. The information concerning the use of the program should be thorough with step-by-step commands for performing the operations. There should be numerous examples. Also, a "quick reference card" that describes most commands is helpful. These are extremely useful after students have mastered the basics of the word-processing program. These quick references tend to get misplaced, so several copies should be made. It is good for students to have a copy of the quick reference taped by the computer they are using.

When editing text, clear and helpful headings should appear at the top of the screen. For example, when using *WordPerfect*, by WordPerfect Inc., the headings at the top of the screen include File, Edit, Search, and a few others with pull-down menus. The menus and help features help make the program user friendly.

Another consideration is that incorrect selection of commands should not cause the program to crash. Furthermore, the program should accept abbreviations for common responses. For example, it should accept **N** for no.

Operation of the program should not require the student to turn the computer on and off. The commands should be easy to learn. Use of the program should not require intermittent access to the master word-processing disk. In addition, deleting, moving, underlining, and justification of words, sentences, and paragraphs should be quick and easy. The entire width of the document should appear on the screen. Also it should contain protective features that prevent loss of files and should have simple methods to load, save, and print files.

Summary

All of the attributes of CAI software discussed here are combined into a comprehensive software evaluation form that you have be using throughout this chapter. We encourage you to use and modify this form to meet the needs of your students. Also, you should keep a file of the evaluations that you perform and share them with other teachers.

Research Evaluations

As a master teacher and a professional, you must keep up with the current literature in your specialty. If a you are going to use CAI software in your classroom, then you should look at what the current research literature says about CAI software. In the literature, you will find the most recent methods for using CAI software to best benefit students. Often, the research literature will contain information about the use of specific CAI packages.

The list of journals and magazines in Figure 3.5 is an excellent starting point. For example, the Spring 1992 issue (vol. 24, no. 3) of *Teaching Exceptional Children* contains the article "Selecting Age-Appropriate Software" by Gardner, Taber-Brown, and Wissick. In this article, the authors give suggestions for selecting age-appropriate software for adolescents and adults with developmental disabilities. The authors discuss age-appropriate CAI, sources of this type of software, and screening and evaluating software. At the end of the article, a list of selected software information resources is given. Another example is in the Spring 1991 issue (vol. 23, no. 3) of the same journal. This issue contains an article by Malouf, Jamison, Kercher, and Carlucci, entitled "Integrating Computer Software into Effective Instruction," that discusses topics such as teacher monitoring, limiting errors, pacing, and remedial feedback.

In addition to general information, the research and conference literature also contain information concerning the use of specific CAI software. The spring 1989 issue of *Teaching Exceptional Children* discusses how teachers can use the program *AppleWorks* to improve their productivity. It tells the teacher how to use the program to monitor student progress, how to use it as a gradebook, and how to use it to prepare lessons.

At the annual meeting of the Council for Learning Disabilities in Baltimore, Maryland, in October of 1993, Patricia Shubert and Mindy Williams held a session titled "Co-Teaching with Computers." In their presentation, Shubert and Williams discussed CAI software used with students and software that they used in preparation of their lessons. For example, they discussed their use of *Bankstreet Writer for the MAC* by Scholastic and *World Geograph* by MECC. In addition to these CAI packages, they discussed their use of MECC's *Vocabulary Series* in their classrooms. Furthermore, Shubert and Williams said that they felt the best way to integrate technology was to use technology for making study guides and tests. The software that they used for these two tasks were *Study Guide* by MECC and *Study Mate* by Compu Teach. They also pointed out that desktop publishing software can be easily used to do worksheets on an individual basis.

In summary, we encourage master teachers to use the research and conference literature as sources of information on CAI software. No one person can cover all possible sources, but a local group or organization of interested teachers can disseminate information to each other from the literature, if each person keeps up with one or two sources of literature and shares any information found.

Conclusion

In this chapter, we discussed the aspects of your hardware that are essential to purchase software. Furthermore, we gave detailed instructions on how to obtain this information. We then discussed software. In particular, we placed a tremendous emphasis on evaluation of software. Total evaluation of software includes the use of both applications and research evaluations. Teachers should use research evaluations and external applications evaluations for initial screening of software. They should then use Form 3.3 to perform an internal applications evaluation.

References

Bitter, G. G., Camuse, R. A., & Durbin, V. L. (1993). *Using a Microcomputer in the Classroom* (3rd ed.). Boston: Allyn and Bacon.

Gardner, J. E., Taber-Brown, F. M., & Wissick, C. A. (1992). Selecting Age-Appropriate Software for Adolescents and Adults with Developmental Disabilities. *Teaching Exceptional Children*, 24(3), 60–63.

Lewis, R. B. (1993). *Special Education Technology: Classroom Applications*. Pacific Grove, CA: Brooks/Cole Publishing.

Maddux, C. D., Johnson, D. L., & Willis, J. W. (1992). *Educational Computing: Learning with Tomorrow's Technologies*. Boston: Allyn and Bacon.

Malouf, D. B., Jamison, P. J., Kercher, M. H., & Carlucci, C. M. (1991). Computer Software Aids Effective Instruction. *Teaching Exceptional Children*, 23(2), 56–57.

Malouf, D. B., Jamison, P. J., Kercher, M. H., & Carlucci, C. M. (1991). Integrating Computer Software into Effective Instruction. *Teaching Exceptional Children*, 23(3), 54–56.

Malouf, D. B., Jamison, P. J., Kercher, M. H., & Carlucci, C. M. (1991). Integrating Computer Software into Effective Instruction (Part 2). *Teaching Exceptional Children*, 23(4), 57–60.

Vockell, E. L., & Mihail, T. (1993). Principles Behind Computerized Instruction for Students with Exceptionalities. *Teaching Exceptional Children*, (25)3, 39–43.

4

Students and Computers

Renet L. Bender

*U*pon completion of this chapter you should be able to:

◆ Make informed decisions concerning computers in your classroom.

◆ Identify instructional options for computers.

◆ Identify computer applications in daily life.

One key to effective utilization of computers and CAI software in the classroom is organization (Littauer, 1994). In this chapter, we will begin by addressing three areas where organization can considerably enhance the quality and enjoyment of computers. The first area addresses the *mechanics of student use* of computers in the classroom. This area includes such basic information as the placement of computers and the scheduling of students and computers. Scheduling computer time includes a discussion on how frequently students should use computers in order to feel comfortable with them. Teaching students to use computers is one of the most important things teachers can do for students. These lessons will stay with the students for the rest of their lives. Instructing students about computer use includes teaching them keyboard skills, how to use menus, and techniques to reduce stress when using computers.

The second area is *instructional options* for the classroom. This area includes a review of basic instructional principles, suggestions for computer use in the classroom, the basics of how to fully integrate CAI software into lessons, and lesson options. Lesson options are the modifications that teachers can make to software to individualize it for particular students. These options allow for much greater flexibility in software use and greatly enhance the overall usefulness of the software.

The third area concerns the *applications of computer knowledge* taken from the classroom into everyday life. If at all possible, the classroom should prepare at-risk students for the types of technology they will be expected to use in their daily lives and at the workplace, such as automatic teller machines (ATMs), informational computers, computerized phone systems, and business software.

Using Computers in the Classroom

When considering how to use computers in the classroom, there are several implementation issues that need to be addressed. These include the physical placement of the computer(s), the integration of computers into the curriculum, and teaching students how to use computers.

Placement of Computers

Lewis (1993), and Bitter, Camuse, and Durbin (1993) suggest that the computer be placed at the side or back of the classroom (it should be in the back of the classroom only if the classroom is not too deep). This placement is preferable for several reasons:

1. The teacher needs to be able to monitor the students when they are using the computer while still leading instruction elsewhere in the class. If the computer is placed in a cubby hole, the teacher may be unable to see what is happening at the computer.
2. Graphics and sound from the computer and software can be distracting to the other students. A pair of headphones is recommended so the rest of the class will not hear the sounds. Most teachers place the computer on the side of the classroom and either turn the sound off or instruct the students to use headphones. Headphones are available only for computers that have sound boards with speakers or speech synthesizers.
3. The computer should not be placed so the entire class can see an error that the student makes, which might be embarrassing to the student.
4. Side placement, along the walls, also serves to protect the computer, more so than central placement. If overtly aggressive behavior does erupt in the class, resulting in overturned centrally located desks, you certainly do not want the computer to be on them.
5. Most classrooms have electrical outlets located on the walls.

Scheduling Computer Time

Scheduling computer time varies considerably depending on a student's disabilities and the size of the class. For example, if a student has a difficult time staying on task, a teacher would not want to schedule that student for 30 minutes of computer time. Instead, he or she could be scheduled for three blocks of 10 to 15 minutes of computer time, separating the computer time by other noncomputer activities. Another option would be to schedule that student, along with a peer tutor, for 30 minutes of CAI time.

Many at-risk students have difficulties remembering what they are supposed to do with the computer, unless these skills are practiced frequently. If students feel confident in their abilities to use the computer, then it will be easier to have them work with a computer. Therefore, at-risk students will probably do better if they have contact with the computer each day, or perhaps twice a day. If there is only one computer in the classroom, schedule the students as frequently as possible, perhaps for 10 to 15 minutes every other day, depending on their disabilities and the number of students. This will be much more effective than 30 to 45 minutes once a week, and it will also help make the students more comfortable with working on their own on the computer. Also, the time spent monitoring CAI use will decrease as the students' confidence grows.

When students are comfortable using CAI software, the teacher can post a written CAI schedule on the wall and let the students be responsible for using the computer and CAI when they are scheduled. The teacher can also make students responsible for monitoring their CAI time and quitting on time.

The activity in Try This 4.1 is designed to help with scheduling students for using the computer. If you already have some sort of scheduling form, you may wish to skip this activity.

> ***Try This 4.1*** *Form 4.1 shows a form for scheduling students on the computer. Try using this form in your classroom. If your students do not have reading skills, you can use pictures and a digital clock on a poster-size copy of this form.*

Teaching Students to Use the Computer

In this section, we discuss several aspects of using a computer. First, we present some fun suggestions on how to teach students keyboard skills. Several software packages are also available to help with this task. Next, we present a strategy to help students with poor fine motor coordination. The last topic in this section is how to teach students the mechanics of computer use. This involves turning the computer on, loading the software, reminding students of the steps in using the computer, and reviewing a software package that makes this task a little easier for teachers and students.

Keyboard Skills

Keyboard skills are very important when using instructional software (Lewis, 1993; Bitter, Camuse, & Durbin, 1993). Lack of these skills can cause students to become frustrated at the time it takes to perform a task. However, keyboard skills should not be a prerequisite for computer use. As students use computers more frequently, the need for keyboard skills will become apparent to them as they become frustrated by having to hunt for keys. They will then become more motivated to learn these skills.

When young students start using CAI, one of the first things they learn is that in order to communicate with the computer, one uses a keyboard. Most programs for very young students use only a few keys: the Enter or Return key, the spacebar, and the arrow keys. It is only when students begin to use the computer for writing that they must learn the location of the letter keys. When students are first learning to use the keyboard, it may be beneficial to use an alternative keyboard, such as *IntelliKeys* or *Muppet Learning Keys*, that arranges the keys in alphabetical order. At some point, however, students must use standard keyboards that have the QWERTY or standard configuration.

Students with early grade-level skills usually begin to interact with the computer using the *hunt-and-peck* method on the keyboard. Some of these students will become very adept in this method. However, if one long-term goal is for your students to use word-processing software, then they should be taught a quick and efficient method with which to interact with the keyboard. Touch-typing, where students learn the location of keys on the keyboard by touch, is the most efficient keyboard method for most students.

The problem that many teachers face is that teaching touch-typing to students requires time, usually at the expense of other subjects. One possible solution is to teach touch-typing as a part of the writing curriculum (Lewis, 1993). For instance, you may have the students perform their writing assignments on

FORM 4.1
Computer Schedule

Day _____

Student Name	CAI to Use	Start Time	End Time

the computer using a word-processing package and mark 3 to 5 minutes of the lesson time for instruction in touch-typing. It is exciting for students to learn locations of keys and then immediately use these keys in the writing lesson. Furthermore, Bitter, Camuse, and Durbin (1993) suggest that older students should attend personal or business typing classes offered by schools. The standard method of teaching typing in these classes is touch-typing.

The activity in Try This 4.2 is designed to help students practice with just a few keys that they have learned. If you are already instructing students in keyboard skills, you may wish to skip this activity.

> ***Try This 4.2*** *Design a writing assignment around a few keys on the keyboard. First, teach the students these keys by touch-typing, then give them a writing assignment that consists of one paragraph that is already written and ask the students to add to the story using these keys. The writing assignment consists of having the students write the paragraph that is already done on the computer and adding their own part. Figure 4.1 gives an example of this type of lesson and Form 4.2 is provided to help with this.*

FORM 4.2
Writing Lessons Using Specific Keys

Keys to practice touch-typing: _____

Story topic: _____

_____

Beginning of the story: _____

_____

_____

_____

_____

_____

_____

FIGURE 4.1 *Key Practice Lesson*

Keys: Practice touch typing using the keys ASDFJKL.

Story Topic: SAD LAD

Beginning Paragraph: JJ's

 JJ is a sad sad lad. JJs Dad is sad. Sad sad sad.

The teaching of keyboard skills can begin with young students, as soon as their hands are big enough to comfortably reach the keys. Until their hands are big enough, there are several options: a touch screen, a mouse, or a specially designed keyboard for young students, all of which are discussed in Chapter 3. Also, small children may use the hunt-and-peck method.

When students are big enough to learn keyboard skills, they should be taught that the fingers of the left hand are placed on the ASDF keys and those of the right hand on the JKL; keys. This particular row of keys is called the *home row*. The students' thumbs should rest lightly on the spacebar. From this position, students will learn the remainder of the keys.

There are software packages that are available to help teach students keyboard skills. Most of this software starts by demonstrating and/or describing how each key should be pressed. Some of these programs show a keyboard on the screen and demonstrate keystrokes by highlighting specific keys. As the students practice with these new keys, they receive immediate feedback on their accuracy. A few of the programs do not accept an incorrect keystroke. Generally, programs that teach keyboard skills usually contain practice drills that emphasize accuracy and speed. Most keep a record of each student's performance so the student and the teacher can see how the student is improving.

One example of a software package to teach young students keyboard skills is *Type to Learn* by Sunburst Communications. This software is available for Apple, Macintosh, IBM, and IBM compatible computers. *Type to Learn* uses pictures of two hands on the computer screen to demonstrate the key strokes to students. The fingers on the computer screen wait for the student to follow them before moving to the next key stroke. Most directions are given as words and symbols, so the program can be used with prereaders.

This program is easy to use with its menus and appealing graphics. The main menu displays five options. The first option is "Learn New Keys," which teaches students new keys. The second is "Games," which contains games to reinforce the new keys the student has learned. The next is "Scratch Pad," which is a simplified word processor that allows the student to use only the keys that have been mastered so far in the lessons. The fourth is "Speed Up," which provides text at the top of the screen for the student to copy. The final option is "Good-bye," which exits from the program.

Type to Learn uses colorful graphics and an errorless learning feature to keep students motivated. It also has a teacher management option that allows teachers to individualize and maintain records using a Change Option menu. This program comes with a detailed manual explaining all parts of the program. The manual also includes a section for teachers with suggestions for using *Type to Learn* in their classrooms, and a section for use with exceptional students, including gifted students. The manual contains numerous forms and charts to use and detailed write-ups of the lessons.

Junior Typer by Aquarius Instructional is another program that teaches keyboard skills. This software is available for Apple, Macintosh, IBM, and IBM compatible computers, and it can also be purchased through Edmark. *Junior Typer* uses the techniques of showing a keyboard on the screen and demonstrating the keystrokes to facilitate exercises for letter combinations, numbers, word-phrase combinations, and sentences. This program uses menus that allow the teacher to choose the skills on which the students need practice. Furthermore, each student's progress is tested and recorded. This program is appropriate for the skill level of elementary grades.

Another software program for students at the kindergarten through eighth-grade skill level is *Talking Fingers* by California Neuropsychology Services (marketed by Cambridge Development Laboratory in the *Special Times*, discussed in Appendix II). This program uses speech sound with a finger stroke on the keyboard to teach students not only keyboard skills but also word processing and phonics. The software consists of several parts. One part, "Typing Challenges," uses graphics that display two imaginary keyboard houses with rooms on different floors (representing the rows of keys) inhabited by characters. These characters come alive to guide students through the mystery of the keyboard. Another part of this software package, "Discovery Textwriter," is a talking word processor that can be used with students who are just learning to read. *Talking Fingers* is currently available for use with Apple, Macintosh, IBM, and IBM compatible computers.

Yet another program that is widely used is *Mavis Beacon Teaches Typing!* (Apple, Macintosh, IBM, and IBM compatible computers) by Software Toolworks (marketed by Cambridge Development Laboratory in the *Special Times*, discussed in Appendix II).

These various software packages are just a sample of the many packages on the market designed to help students, at all skill levels, learn keyboard skills. You should keep in mind that the use of computer software to teach keyboard skills is just one teaching method. The addresses for the companies mentioned in the previous paragraphs can be found in Appendix II.

Other methods of teaching keyboard skills include the use of "pseudo"-keyboards, music, and taping letters to students' fingers. A pseudo-keyboard is a piece of paper or cloth upon which is drawn a keyboard. These pseudo-keyboards are easy and inexpensive to make and are ideal for teaching the entire class or groups of students touch typing when the number of computers in the classroom is limited. Another advantage of having pseudo-keyboards is that the students can take them home and practice. Using music with touch-typing practice can be exciting to students. In these drills, the students press the keys of the practice drill in time with the music.

Another suggestion is to use washable ink to tape or write letters on the students fingers so that they can remember which keys get pressed by which fingers. For example, Figure 4.2 shows which fingers are used to press which keys. On the student's right index finger are the letters JHYUMN, and on his or her left middle finger are the letters DEC. This technique helps students remember the position of their fingers on the keyboard. If you use this technique, start with only the letters contained in the home row of the keyboard and then add each row as the student starts to practice on that row.

Most teachers use a combination of the preceding methods to teach touch-typing, based on the learning characteristics of the individual student. No one method or set of methods will be the best for all students, and teachers should experiment with each of these methods for at-risk students.

The activity in Try This 4.3 is designed to help you choose a combination of methods to use in teaching keyboard skills to your class. If you have already found a successful combination, you may wish to skip this activity.

> ***Try This 4.3*** *Use Form 4.3 to list the learning characteristics of your students and to match these characteristics with the methods you feel will best help your students learn keyboard skills. Remember, in the selection of software, your first consideration is the learning characteristics of your students.*

FIGURE 4.2   Lettered Fingers after Learning the Keyboard

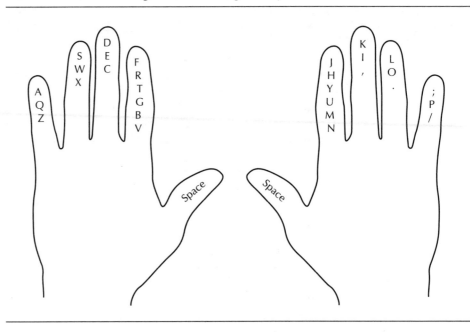

FORM 4.3

Selecting the Best Methods to Teach Your Students Keyboard Skills

On the left-hand side, list the learning characteristics of your students that were discussed in Chapter 2. On the right-hand side, list the keyboard methods that you feel would best help students with that learning characteristic.

Learning Characteristics	**Keyboard Methods**
_____	_____
_____	_____
_____	_____
_____	_____
_____	_____
_____	_____
_____	_____
_____	_____
_____	_____

Can you think of other methods for teaching keyboard skills?

Students with poor fine motor skills may not be able to start directly with a standard keyboard. With these students, you may need to obtain a touch-screen so they can use the computer like the other students while working on their motor skills. It may be helpful to use a modified keyboard whose keys are considerably larger than the keys on a standard keyboard. An example is the *IntelliKeys Expanded Keyboard* by IntelliTools, which is discussed in Chapter 3. This keyboard is a flat surface marked off in squares. The teacher can combine any number of squares to form a particular key. *IntelliKeys* requires no extra hardware and comes with a complete step-by-step manual for installation. This keyboard does require special software to program which squares will be which keys. After the student has mastered the modified keyboard, he or she should move to a standard keyboard. At no time should a student's lack of fine motor skills prevent him or her from working on computers like the other students.

Teaching Students the Basics

Having good keyboard skills alone is not sufficient for students to feel confident in using a computer; they also must know how to use a computer properly. This learning experience can be both frightening and exciting to at-risk students. Everyone at one time or another has forgotten how to do a simple task on a computer or give a particular command. The goals of this and the next few sections are to present methods for teaching students how to operate a computer and to help students remember the steps in its operation. In short, if a student forgets a step in the operation of a computer, the teacher wants to use methods that allow that student to "look up" what to do. This is an aspect of computer use that is often overlooked in computer applications instruction for students at all levels. Nevertheless, this is one of the most important aspects of computer use. If the students can solve their own problems, then the teacher will have more time to concentrate on other things. Obviously, this ability to problem solve fosters student independence as well as self-confidence about using computers.

In using computers, there are several basic steps that must be taught to students regardless of the system used. These basic steps are:

1. *Turn on the computer and the monitor.* Some computers and monitors have their power switches in obscure places. Others are plugged into a power bar (a portable outlet that has 6 to 10 plug-ins) that also has an on-off switch. Students must do this as a first step.

2. *Adjust the contrast and brightness of the monitor.* These dials are easily changed by curious students and by anyone cleaning the classroom. Students should be taught to adjust these controls for their comfort.

3. *Put a diskette/CD-ROM in the computer.* Depending on the size of floppy diskettes the system uses, students need to know which side of the floppy disk is the top and how to lock the disk drive. Instruction should also include teaching students how to handle floppy disks and CD-ROMs. For example, students should be taught not to touch the actual disk and to handle the CD-ROMs on the edge. They are going to be curious about what a floppy disk looks like inside. Therefore, you should cut one open and have it available for them to inspect. Students should also be taught not to leave floppy diskettes in the sun—they may melt. You may wish to demonstrate this to them; take one outside during a hot day and show them the result. Further-

more, your students need to know if a diskette is required in the disk drive before they turn the power on (this is true for older computers).

Computer Operator's License

When teaching students how to operate a computer, some teachers issue what is called an operator's license, which is similar to a driver's license (Lewis, 1993). With this method, the students are individually shown how to operate the computer. They practice for awhile and then, when they feel they are ready, they demonstrate their ability to operate the computer. For some at-risk students, teachers may wish to have them demonstrate their new skills for the entire class, to help them build confidence. Upon the successful completion of the "licensing" test, students are awarded their operator's licenses. Figure 4.3 is an example of such a license.

Computer Instructions Chart

Because many at-risk students demonstrate memory problems, teachers should place a computer instructions chart nearby that reminds students of the basic steps in using the computer. These charts can take several forms. For example, if the students have reading skills, then the teacher can make a poster that enumerates the steps and hang it on the wall behind the computer. Figure 4.4 is an example of such a chart. If writing the basic steps is not appropriate for students, the teacher may wish to make a poster using pictures (these are also available from some educational materials companies). One option is to draw pictures of the steps—for example, draw the power switch and use an arrow to indicate which way the students are supposed to push it, and draw a picture of a floppy diskette being placed in the disk drive.

FIGURE 4.3 *Computer Operator's License*

Name: _____

Date: _____

Computer: _____

Sign off on each of the steps of operation as the student demonstrates his or her proficiency.

1. _____

2. _____

3. _____

4. _____

I hereby certify that _____ has demonstrated the ability to operate a computer. I hereby

authorize _____ to use the computer.

Date _____

Signature _____

Source: From *Special Education Technology: Classroom Applications* by R. B. Lewis. Copyright © 1993 Wadsworth, Inc. Reprinted by permission of Brooks/Cole Publishing Company, Pacific Grove, CA 93950.

FIGURE 4.4 *Computer Instructions Chart*

At the Beginning

1. Put the disk in the disk drive (the slot in the front of the computer).
   The top side goes up. (The top is the side with the label.)
   The metal part goes in first.
2. Turn on the computer.
   The switch is on the back right and you push it up.
3. Turn on the monitor.
   The switch is on the front right and you push it.
4. Adjust the contrast and brightness.
   These knobs are blue and are on the front of the monitor.

At the End

1. When finished, take the disk out of the disk drive.
   (Press the blue button under the disk drive.)
2. Turn the computer off.
3. Turn the monitor off.
4. Replace the software in its proper place.

The teacher may also cut pictures out of magazines or use actual snapshots of students performing these tasks. No matter which option is chosen, the basic steps in some form should be posted by the computer so if a student forgets these steps, he or she will not be upset or embarrassed.

Software Organization

The final aspect of teaching students to use a computer is setting up the software so that the student does not need the teacher's help to begin a CAI assignment. The strategy that is chosen should be based on the skill level of the students. We discuss here several methods for organizing software; teachers should combine these methods as necessary.

First, we will focus on some ideas for students who have not mastered reading. One suggestion is to color code the software (Lewis, 1993). For example, the teacher could put blue dots on one specific program (i.e., put blue dots on the disks, the manual, and anything else that goes with that software). He or she could then place a chart on the wall that has the students' names or pictures and the same color dots as those on the students' software. When a teacher wants a student to work on the computer with a particular software program, he or she tells the student to use the correctly colored software. The problem with this suggestion is the restriction in the number of software programs that can be used, because of the rather limited availability of colors. A solution to this problem is to use a combination of color coding and students' names or pictures. In this case, each box of software would not only have a color associated with it but also a list of names or pictures. If a teacher uses this method, the software could be arranged on the shelves by color. For instance, all the red color-coded software could be on one shelf all the green on another, and so on. Also, pictures of the students could be placed near or on the appropriate software.

Another suggestion for students at this skill level is to create a folder for each student. In that folder, the teacher would place copies of either the cover of the manual or the box for particular software the student will use. The student would then have to match the copied page with the actual manual cover or the box of the software. When using this option, the teacher will need to show at-risk students how to match these pages to the actual software.

As you can see, the "color plus picture" option can become cumbersome, and you may wonder if there is a CAI program available to help match students with the correct software. You will be pleased to know that a recent option for teachers that have computers with hard drives is *KidDesk* (Macintosh, IBM, and IBM compatible computers) by Edmark. This program functions as an interface between the student and the computer, which makes using the computer easier. Using *KidDesk,* the teacher can control which individual programs on the hard drive that students can use. The teacher creates an icon on the main screen for each student who is to use the computer and decides to which programs that student may have access. The student gains access to programs by clicking the mouse on his or her icon. He or she will then see another screen containing icons for the software that he or she is allowed to use. All student choices in *KidDesk* are graphical and require no reading skills. Using *KidDesk,* students can run software programs or explore interactive desk accessories, which include a talking clock, an interactive calendar, a working calculator, and a message machine.

Notebook of CAI Use

If students have minimal reading skills, then in addition to the preceding options, the teacher can create a notebook for them. To create a notebook, the teacher should include one page for each CAI package that the student is using. The student should use the notebook to keep a record of his or her performance with each software package. (The teacher may have to encourage students to make notes about the software packages in their notebooks.)

It is extremely important for students to realize that all software is different and computers are different. If a student is having difficulty in the use of a software package on a computer, have the student make a note in his or her notebook concerning this difficulty, including thoughts on how to avoid the difficulty in the future. This teaches students a valuable problem-solving skill. If they encounter a problem, they should check their notebooks to see if they have had this problem before. If they *have* experienced this problem, then they can read in their notebooks what to do; if not, then they should call the teacher, solve the problem, and then write notes on how to solve the problem in the future. This will dramatically decrease the number of students asking the teacher the same questions over and over.

The teacher may want to have the students break into groups once a month and share what problems they have encountered and their solutions with the group. Keeping a notebook that contains notes on how to use different computer systems and software is a common practice in industry and business where there is interaction with numerous types of systems. While it is not realistic to expect all students to enjoy their "notebook" activity, a few at-risk students will become quite adept at identifying and solving these types of problems. Some may begin to help others solve CAI problems. We know of one special education classroom in which a student with learning disabilities became the class "problem solver" based on this notebook idea. He gained both self-respect and confidence as he helped other students (and on occasion, the teacher) with their computer use problems.

Instructional Options for the Classroom

We have discussed the use of computers in the classroom with respect to the placement of and scheduling of time on computers. Furthermore, we have also remarked on the student skills that make computer usage more comfortable for teachers and students. In this section, we will discuss suggestions on instructional use of CAI software in the classroom.

Effective Instructional Principles

The instructional options for at-risk students are virtually endless if the use of CAI is well grounded in effective learning principles (Malouf, Jamison, Kercher, & Carlucci, 1991; Vockell & Mihail, 1993). This foundation for effective CAI utilization was discussed in Chapter 2, in terms of provision of feedback, pacing, errorless learning, and immediate reinforcement. Vockell and Mihail (1993) and Malouf, Jamison, Kercher, and Carlucci (1991) present detailed sets of

TABLE 4.1   Guidelines for Implementation of CAI

Mastery Practice	Pacing	Immediate Feedback
1. Use programs that specify exact steps and teach them clearly and specifically.	1. Use computer programs to provide self-paced individualized practice.	1. Use programs that provide immediate feedback.
2. Show the relationship of computer programs to steps in the direct instruction process.	2. Use computer programs that provide game-like practice for skills that require much repeated practice.	2. Use programs that provide clear corrective feedback.
3. Use programs that provide extra help and practice toward reaching objectives.	3. Use computer programs that provide varied approaches to practicing the same activity.	3. Select programs that ask higher-level questions.
4. Use programs to stimulate and enrich students who reach objectives early.	4. Use programs that individualize the pace of instruction, since wait time is likely to be better than with traditional instruction.	4. Use programs that have management systems to monitor student progress.
5. Use record-keeping programs to keep track of student performance.		5. Use record-keeping programs.
6. Use computer programs to provide repeated practice and to facilitate memorization.		6. Use computers to communicate feedback.
7. Use programs designed to develop memory skills.		7. Teach students to use the computer as a tool to manage and assist learning.
		8. Use programs that teach thinking skills.
		9. Teach generalization of thinking and study skills across subject areas.

guidelines for implementation of computer-assisted instruction for at-risk students. The synopsis in Table 4.1 comes from these and other sources.

Within the context of these effective instructional principles, CAI can be applied to numerous learning problems demonstrated by at-risk students. Further, research has demonstrated that appropriate use of CAI is at least as effective as the whole group instruction that is typically provided in most public school classes (Perry & Garber, 1993; Raskind, 1993; van Daal & van der Leij, 1992). The effective teacher will implement CAI instruction with these guidelines in mind by concentrating on the particular learning characteristics of the student in question.

Computers in the Classroom

A number of researchers have begun to highlight what computer-assisted instruction and computer-enhanced capabilities can offer to the student who is at-risk (Perry & Garber, 1993; Raskind, 1993). The word-processing options were discussed previously, though those instructional packages comprise only a small part of what computers can offer.

Spelling Instruction

Spelling difficulties can be addressed in at least two ways using computers: spell-check programs and CAI for spelling instruction. Raskind (1993) indicated that the spell-checking option was particularly useful for students who have spelling difficulty. These programs, when implemented, automatically scan the student's written text, comparing the words in the text with words in the spell-check memory. When a match is not found, the computer alerts the writer that an error may have been made. The student can then look up the word or select a word from the option of choices presented on screen by the spell-check program. As Raskind (1993) indicates, that type of selection of a correctly spelled word may be problematic for some students with learning disabilities, since visual scanning of a word list may be a weakness for some students. However, the use of spell-checking programs is certainly one option that teachers should offer to students on their written work.

A spelling program was used to instruct 28 students with written language disorders in a study by van Daal and van der Leij (1992). In that study, the computer kept a record of pupil errors, and students were instructed to copy the errors from the computer screen. CAI instructional practice was found to result in fewer spelling errors than other paper and pencil techniques, demonstrating the effectiveness of CAI as an instructional tool.

Proofreading Programs

Numerous teachers have indicated that use of proofreading programs can enhance writing skills for at-risk students (Raskind, 1993; Vockell & Mihail, 1993). Computer packages can check for many common errors in a student's written work, such as punctuation (e.g., periods, commas, and missing question marks), grammar (e.g., subject and verb agreement), capitalization, and word usage (Raskind, 1993). Some programs merely highlight the suspected error, whereas other programs actually provide a tutorial for the particular example. However, unlike spelling errors, errors in grammar and word usage are much more difficult to detect and interpret, and research has indicated that these proofreading programs make numerous errors (Frankel, 1990). In spite of this drawback, these proofreading programs can work for many students who are at-risk. For example, some students detest writing (probably since they have not written successfully before), and proofreading programs may allow those students to turn in work that is much improved over work they could have done without the use of such programs.

Outlining Programs

Programs that assist a student in outlining his or her ideas can increase the student's written output. With these programs, students are free to brainstorm and get their thoughts down in an unstructured manner without worry that the ideas will be lost. The computer program will then assist the student in formation of meaningful relationships between the ideas (Raskind, 1993). These programs allow for placement of ideas together, if they seem to fit together. Also, the programs allow for moving the ideas into other superordinate or subordinate relationships if, upon reflection, the first idea configuration doesn't work out.

These various programs can assist at-risk students who seem to have difficulty in idea organization in their written work. Many students with mental retardation or learning disabilities demonstrate these problems. One method to use this CAI is to let the at-risk student formulate the outline which, when perfected, becomes the basis for the class discussion. This allows the at-risk student to have a successful educational experience, shared with the rest of the class.

Some teachers have used these outlining programs to provide an alternative type of assessment in secondary area content classes. The teacher could present the student with 25 or 30 outline headings/statements and instruct the student to place the ideas in relationship to each other. This CAI application would be particularly useful in secondary programs where numerous hierarchial orderings are possible for certain material such as history and science. Students should be encouraged to explain their rationale for the selected outline format.

Speech Synthesizers and Speech Recognition Systems

Numerous researchers have indicated that CAI, coupled with speech recognition and speech synthesizer systems, can assist students who are at-risk in a number of ways (Montague & Fonseca, 1993; Raskind, 1993). As indicated in an earlier chapter, many classroom computer systems now include a speech synthesizer. This allows students with reading programs to access the computer and read along with a computerized narrator. Speech can be read back in small sections—or even one word, sentence, or paragraph—at a time. This type of brief review, coupled with the requirement that the at-risk student write down the main idea of each paragraph in text before proceeding to the next paragraph, can greatly enhance a student's comprehension. This CAI technique would be appropriate from about the second- or third-grade reading level throughout the secondary school years.

When coupled with an optical scanner (which actually takes text from the printed page and puts it inside the computer), a speech synthesizer becomes a powerful teaching tool (Raskind, 1993). For example, some at-risk students have difficulty reading print but have no difficulty in understanding what is read to them. A scanning device—which can translate any printed page into the computer—coupled with the speech synthesizer allows that student to hear every reading assignment in the secondary school program. If only one such system was available at every secondary school, this would greatly enhance the education of numerous at-risk students.

The talking calculators that are currently available on the market utilize built-in speech synthesizers and represent another variation on this theme. Some students need to hear material rather than read it in order to facilitate adequate comprehension (Raskind, 1993). These talking systems can make that learning mode quite possible.

It is widely recognized that word-processing systems can facilitate the writing process, since reluctant writers are typically encouraged to write a great deal more and to worry about revisions and errors later (Montague & Fonseca, 1993). However, even in the initial stages of writing, computers can help. Raskind (1993) described a sophisticated system that would actually recognize the speech generated by students and translate that speech into written text. Students must be instructed to speak slowly into a microphone. The system selects the word from memory and prints it on the screen. The student must then check to see that the correct word was selected. Some systems of this nature can take dictation of 40 to 70 words per minute (Raskind, 1993). Systems such as this would greatly benefit reluctant writers.

Although these sophisticated systems are not widely available in public school classrooms today, these systems do indicate the potential for computerized enhancement of current instructional endeavors. With the cost of this technology decreasing, these systems should be more widely available in the future.

Fundamental Mathematics

Difficulties in mathematics can be addressed with CAI software. Lubke, Roger, and Evans (1989) used a multimedia program to teach fractions. The results were encouraging in that the students remained motivated and enjoyed working with the program. The students were not as apprehensive about mathematics since the multimedia program allowed them to review instructional sequences at any time. If they forgot how to do something, they could review the material. In fact, Bottge and Hasselbring (1993) used a multimedia program to teach problem solving in mathematics. Their study showed that with carefully chosen CAI software, students can improve substantially more than students who are taught the standard paper and pencil methods.

In the general classroom setting, students usually differ in where they are having problems. Mathematics CAI software can tutor students individually or in groups requiring minimal teacher monitoring. Woodward and Howard (1994) are developing a technology-based advanced diagnostic system, called *TORUS*, for examining and remedying mathematical misconceptions of students. Widespread use of systems such as these and CAI software in mathematics can quickly notice and correct misconceptions before they become major stumbling blocks to mathematics.

Personal Data Managers

Many at-risk students demonstrate not only academic difficulties but also organizational difficulties. Teachers are quite able to state to any class visitor which students in the class are likely to come in without their books or with the wrong page done from last night's homework assignment. These problems sometimes represent a lack of motivation, but they may also represent an innate inability to organize. We have talked to numerous adults with attention deficit disorders and learning disabilities who demonstrate these problems and have learned to compensate for them with a computerized organizational system. Such programs exist for both laptop computers and hand-held units, and may include monthly calendars, daily schedules, planners, appointments, memo files, and so on (Raskind, 1993). Applications of this technology for many at-risk students in this nation's middle and secondary schools would result in a drastic increase in the amount of homework and long-term class projects that are completed and turned in on time.

Utilization of These Systems

This book can only alert you, the teacher, to the possibilities that exist or are on the horizon. You should check with the media person in your school concerning which of these types of systems may be available for student use. Further, over the long term, you should try to obtain these types of systems for your classroom and/or school. Although these systems will not solve all the educational problems of at-risk students, there are very few learning characteristics for which some CAI solution is not available. Like all instructional ideas, these approaches will work for some students and not for others, but CAI of this nature should be included in the arsenal of every master teacher.

Inclusive Instruction with CAI

Inclusion has many different meanings to different people. Generally, most would agree that *inclusion* is placing students with disabilities into mainstream classes, and having the special education teacher co-teach those mainstream classes for some period of the school day. While a debate of the wisdom on inclusion is beyond the scope of this book, inclusive instruction is ongoing around the country. One question thus becomes, How can inclusion be facilitated using CAI, when most classrooms have only one computer (if that!)? Fortunately, a number of computer simulations have been marketed for cooperative instruction by Tom Snyder Productions, Inc. This company has a number of interactive simulation games in various subject areas that are basically dependent on the "jigsaw" format, in which the various role-play participants are each given limited information and a perspective about a particular problem.

Duke and Rumpp (1994) described an interactive simulation involving the waste problems associated with a local dump and a fish kill in the local pond. The program, titled "The Environment," is available for Macintosh, Apple, and MS–Dos formats. It is recommended for grades 5 through 12. Role-play descriptions were provided for an economist, an environmentalist, the campaign manager for the local mayor, and a scientist, who participated in a structured series of lessons to develop an action plan to solve the problem. The lessons are flexible enough such that this simulation could be completed in two to three days, or could become the basis for an entire unit of instruction, which would be appropriate for either a science or a social studies class.

Both teachers (Duke & Rumpp, 1994) had utilized this simulation in an inclusive classroom and had placed students with disabilities into the role-play groups along with the other students. In cooperative situations such as this, the CAI is a support for students with reading difficulties, since they may not be able to read their role-play descriptions as well as other students. More importantly, as many as five to seven groups may be formed within the same classroom, and as different decisions are made, the groups go in different directions at each point in the simulation. With only one computer, the class can pursue the different simulation agendas of numerous groups, and students with disabilities are included in each group. The teachers did indicate that students with disabilities should not be placed in the same group and that groups basically should be compared on how well they meet their objectives only if the groups are formed at roughly equal levels. Still, a number of simulations are available, and these will facilitate use of CAI in large inclusive classrooms, which is good news for teachers who are committed to both use of technology and inclusive instruction.

Integration of CAI

As mentioned previously, computers are at their best when they are integrated into the classroom. Also, research has shown that CAI is very effective if it is properly evaluated, modified, and integrated into the classroom (Malouf, Jamison, Kercher, & Carlucci, 1991; Gardner, Taber-Brown, & Wissick, 1992). Appropriate modification of software should facilitate the integration into the curriculum. The following suggestions should help teachers modify and integrate CAI into their classroom in a reasonable amount of time and without stress on either teachers or students.

1. To begin, select one program or software package that is appropriate for several students. Modify this software as needed for the chosen students. This may be as simple as increasing the time allowed for responses or typing in the students' names. Decide on an appropriate amount of time for the students to use this software in one sitting. Then select the days of the week that the students should work on this subject and set up a schedule (use Form 4.1). Remember that at-risk students may forget how to use computers if they are not used at least on a bi-weekly basis. Plan your CAI use for several students whom you believe will enjoy the experience. Others in the class will then request their "turn" on the computer.

2. Before moving on to other software, get the bugs out. Evaluate the software. Is it helping the students? Have the students progressed to the next level? Does the software require teacher intervention for a student to have access to the next instructional level? Is the amount of time allotted adequate? Is the student bored or frustrated with the software? You may wish to review the points of software evaluation (discussed in Chapter 3).

3. Move on to other software. After the evaluation questions have been addressed and any problems resolved, choose a second piece of software. Some teachers make the mistake of jumping in with 20 pieces of software and overwork themselves trying to get set up initially. They may become frustrated and cease CAI use altogether. Remember that the computer is a *tool*—not a substitute teacher—and you as the teacher know best how to teach your students. Do not overextend yourself initially. Know the software well.

4. If you have software already in the classroom and do not feel you are using it to its full capabilities, start with a *piece* of the software. Learn more about the software you already have as a first step. Then, after identifying areas in which you would like to use CAI, search for additional software to meet those needs.

5. Spend 10 or 15 minutes every other day before or after class becoming familiar with the CAI programs; modify or evaluate the CAI software as needed. Most software is written so that modifications do not have to be made at one time. Set aside regular times each week to work on integrating soft-

ware into the classroom. This time can be spent individualizing or evaluating software, obtaining software, or evaluating students' performances with the various software they use. A regularly scheduled time will help you become quite familiar with the CAI programs.

6. For older students, require one or two written assignments each week to be completed on a word-processing package. This will help change the students' attitudes toward writing and, in the process, they will become very comfortable with the computer.

Lesson Options

Lesson options are the modifications that the teacher can make to software to individualize it for particular students. Lesson options typically include pacing options, range options, record-keeping options, and skill options. (This is certainly not an exhaustive list.)

Fully utilizing lesson options of software can mean adjusting the skill level of a program or setting up *KidDesk* for your entire class. Teachers should remember that with most CAI software, using lesson options is not necessary in order to use the software. Initially, if you do not have time to consider the lesson options available for a particular CAI program before using it, you should, at a minimum, check that the skill level is appropriate for students. Then, as time is available, use the options in the software to individualize the lessons. One good rule of thumb is to spend 10 minutes every two weeks on your software options; do not spend hours on it because few teachers have that amount of available time. View the time spent on the lesson options of CAI software as an investment. A few minutes here and there will pay off in the long run in helping your students use computers. Also, you will greatly expand the applicability of the software available to you. Following is a discussion on some of the CAI software options commonly available. (These software packages are discussed in either Chapter 2 or Appendix I).

Number Munchers by MECC, discussed in Chapter 2, consists of several games. When using this CAI package, teachers can change some of the game settings. For example, if a teacher does not want students using a certain game, he or she can type NO in the use column for that particular game. Suppose a student is playing a game where the screen consists of 30 squares, each square containing a different addition problem similar in form to "10 + 5". The objective is for the Number Muncher to eat the squares that contain problems that give the same answer as the answer at the top of the screen. For this type of game, the teacher is allowed to restrict answers to a certain range of integers and to specify if the answers are to appear in random order or in increasing order for successive games. Although none of these modifications is required for the CAI program to run, each option may increase the value of the game for particular at-risk students. Therefore, you can start some students using the program, and when you have time make the modifications for other students.

Alligator Mix by DLM, mentioned in Appendix I, allows the teacher to change three game options. The teacher can adjust the skill level (which for this program is the speed at which the problems are presented), problem range (which restricts games to use problems with numbers in a particular range), and run time (which is how long the games last).

Math Blaster Mystery by Davidson consists of four games or activities. Each activity has four skill levels consisting of different types of math problems. For example, one level may consist of double-digit multiplication problems, whereas others are merely single-digit addition problems. These four skill levels vary from activity to activity. The manual explains in detail what the four skill levels for each activity involve. The teacher has the option of setting the skill level or entering other math problems for the students.

Math Shop, Jr. by Scholastic lets the students choose a shop or store to manage and presents math problems to the student. With each customer that comes into the shop, there is a math problem that needs to be solved in order to serve the customer. For one lesson option, students may choose between managing one shop or all the shops at the same time. The teacher may also choose the clock option, where the student is timed when serving customers.

As you can see, lesson options vary widely. Some CAI software has no lesson options (e.g., *Where in the World Is Carmen San Deigo?* by Broderbund) and some give several lesson options. However, all CAI packages will run without any modifications to lesson options. Therefore, when choosing software, teachers may want to look at those packages that are the most flexible (i.e., give the most lesson options). Even if a teacher does not have time to make any modifications initially, modifications at a later time will allow a larger number of students to use the same software.

Technology for Today

In this section, we will discuss the types of technology that at-risk students will use in their everyday lives and at the workplace. If at all possible, the classroom should prepare at-risk students for the types of technology that they will be expected to use.

Technology in Daily Life

The most common computer technology that comes to mind are automatic teller machines (ATMs), price scanners at stores, informational computers in stores or office buildings, and computerized phone systems. If possible, students should not only be exposed to each of these technologies but should also be allowed to practice with them. You can teach students these technologies using field trips and/or demonstrations.

For instance, to teach students about ATMs, teachers may want to take their students on a field trip to a bank and, as part of the trip, show how to use an ATM. The trip to the bank should include telling students how to open and use a checking account, how to keep track of their balance, and how to keep the ATM card safe (e.g., they should not write the personal identification number in a location close to where they keep their card, etc.). The bank manager may assist by explaining the system.

To learn about price scanners at stores, teachers can have their students plan one of their seasonal parties. This would include having the students purchase the food at a grocery store that has bar code scanners. Another suggestion is to go on a field trip to a store that uses computers not only to scan prices and calculate sales but to manage the inventory. The store manager may assist in the presentation.

Informational computers are located at most libraries, malls, government buildings, and some stores. As a homework assignment over a month or so, teachers may have each student (or groups of students) locate and use an informational computer and report to the class about his or her experience. If a teacher chooses to do this assignment, he or she may want to give the students a list of the locations of some informational computers. (If your school is in a small town or rural area, you could videotape yourself or a friend using an informational computer and then show the tape to the class.)

Another example of computer technology in daily life is computerized phone systems. These systems use computers to answer the phone and route the calls to the appropriate person or department. Most government offices, law offices, and medical offices use this technology. If possible, have the students practice with this technology. Instruct them to listen closely to the message and then to press the appropriate button. The teacher will need to explain that these systems work only with tone systems. In other words, these computers expect a sound like a musical note when a button on the telephone is pressed. If the phone is a pulse system, students will hear clicks when a button is pressed. If they are calling from a pulse system, tell the students to stay on the line and a person will eventually answer.

All of these examples of computer technology may seem somewhat trivial to us, but to at-risk students, it may be frightening the first time they use this technology. Encourage the students to practice using these technologies. Find a local number to practice with computerized phone systems. You may be able to enlist the help and support of some local businesses. (Approaching businesses for their help is discussed in Chapter 7.)

The activity in Try This 4.4 is designed as a class project in exploring technology in daily life. If your students are familiar with this technology, you may wish to skip this activity.

> ***Try This 4.4***   *Divide the students into groups and assign one of the technologies mentioned here to each group. Have the groups prepare a presentation on the use of their particular technology for the class. You may even suggest that the presentation include a video demonstration that the students film themselves. This is an excellent project to be worked on over an entire grading period.*

Technology in the Workplace

Computers are extremely common in the work environment. They generally fall into one of two categories: specialized machines or equipment that are run by computers, and general-purpose computers and the software that is commonly used by businesses.

It is difficult to prepare students for using specialized equipment or machines. These skills are usually taught in either vocational-technical schools or on the job. If there is a vocational-technical school or a business nearby that has this type of equipment, try to arrange a field trip with demonstrations of how the operators interact with the equipment. If there is not a place close to your school, call the local hospital's public relations department. Most of the instruments used in medical laboratories and throughout hospitals utilize computers. Most hospitals will be more than happy to arrange a tour and give demonstrations of some of the computerized equipment. The goal of these demonstrations is to make the students aware of how computers can be specialized for the workplace.

The second type of technology in the workplace involves the standard personal computers (PCs) and the types of software that most businesses use. Teachers should want the students to know that there are many different kinds of computers. For example, if there is an older Macintosh in the classroom, see if you can borrow a Power Macintosh to demonstrate to the students. Also, borrow an IBM or an IBM compatible that runs *Windows* and has a CD-ROM drive. Compare how user friendly the different computers are. If you do not have access to different computers, ask if a local computer store or business will demonstrate different computers and allow the students to use them for a few minutes. Inquire if a local business, college, or university has work stations and file servers, and arrange for a tour of its computer facilities with demonstrations. The idea is for students to realize that the computer in their classroom is not the only kind of computer.

The other aspect of computers in the workplace is the software that is used. With this in mind, a major goal of middle, junior high, and high schools should be to teach students the basics of using some of the software packages that are commonly used in the workplace. The students will need a fourth- or fifth-grade skill level in reading and mathematics to learn these packages. All of the packages mentioned here can be run on either Macintosh, IBM, or IBM compatible computers. The software packages most commonly used in the workplace can be classified into four categories: (1) word-processing software, (2) database software, (3) spreadsheets, and (4) accounting software. These four categories of software can be purchased separately or in integrated packages, such as *Microsoft Works* and *Claris Works*. The integrated packages are usually the most cost effective. Furthermore, there is also a large amount of teaching materials available for these integrated packages. When teaching this type of software, most schools only concern themselves with the first three categories of software due to the fact that many businesses have specialized accounting software. Still, the first three types of business programs should be emphasized for at-risk students and adolescents.

Database

A *database* is a collection of items of information about a group of people, places, or things. It typically holds and organizes large amounts of information, or data, and makes any item of information immediately accessible. Most databases are organized into records. Items of information pertaining to a particular person, place, or thing are grouped together to form a record, each of which has the same format. In a database, the user decides what information should be contained in the records. For example, most schools have a database of their students. Each student will have a record, which usually contains the following information:

1. Name
2. Address
3. Social security number
4. Parents' names
5. Place of employment of parents
6. Illnesses the student has
7. Age of student
8. Date of birth of student
9. Grades

Database programs allow the addition, modification, and deletion of records. For example, when a student moves, the school will need to change the address. The special function of databases is information retrieval. Databases are designed so that using "English-like" commands, a person can retrieve any information contained in the records in any order he or she wishes. For example, given the preceding record form, one may retrieve or list all of the students who are 16 years old by the following command:

LIST FOR AGE = 16

Database software is normally priced around $400 to $500, but educators can get a discounted price of around $200. (Faculty identification cards or paycheck stubs are usually sufficient to prove that you are an educator.) There are several databases used by businesses. These include DBASE IV by Borland (IBM and IBM compatible computers), FOXPRO by Microsoft (IBM, IBM compatible, and MacIntosh computers), and PARADOX by Borland (IBM and IBM compatible computers). Databases are also included in the integrated packages *Microsoft Works* and *Claris Works*. When teaching database software to students, we recommend teaching only the basics. Excellent books to use for this include *Using DBASE IV: Software Solutions Series* by Leonard Presby (Houghton Mifflin Company), *10 Minute Guide to Paradox* (SAMS), and *Learn Foxpro in a Day* by Wan M. Wong (Wordware Publications, Inc.). The school office is typically a good place to demonstrate a database by bringing up the students's own record (be careful of confidentiality guidelines here).

Spreadsheets

Spreadsheets are software packages that are used for problems that can be represented in row and column formats. For example, most businesses use spreadsheets for numeric or financial calculations. Furthermore, many spreadsheets have graphic capabilities to do line graphs, bar graphs, pie charts, and so on. An example of a budget done on the spreadsheet software *Lotus 1–2–3* is shown in Figure 4.5, with a bar graph and a pie chart created from the budget shown in Figures 4.6 and 4.7.

Several spreadsheets are commonly found in business, including *Lotus 1–2–3* by Lotus Developmental Corporation (IBM, IBM compatible, and Macintosh), *Excel* by Microsoft (IBM, IBM compatible, and Macintosh), and *Quattropro* by Borland (IBM and IBM compatible). These packages range in price from $50 to $300. Easy-to-read books that teach the basics are *10 Minute Guide for Lotus 1–2–3* and *10 Minute Guide for Excel,* both published by SAMS, and *Quattropro: Easy Series* by Shelley O'Hara (QUE Publishers). All of the *10 Minute Guides* are priced at $10.95 and can be found in most bookstores. Most integrated packages such as *Microsoft Works* and *Claris Works*

FIGURE 4.5 **Renet's Budget**

Expenses	January	February	March	April	May	Totals
Tuition	$1,125.00	$0.00	$0.00	$1,125.00	$0.00	$2,250.00
Books	$200.00	$0.00	$0.00	$180.00	$0.00	$380.00
Rent/Food	$525.00	$525.00	$525.00	$525.00	$525.00	$2,625.00
Entertainment	$100.00	$220.00	$100.00	$100.00	$100.00	$620.00
Car Costs	$250.00	$250.00	$250.00	$250.00	$250.00	$1,250.00
Other Bills	$90.00	$90.00	$90.00	$90.00	$90.00	$450.00
Monthly Expenses	$2,290.00	$1,085.00	$965.00	$2,270.00	$965.00	
Income:						
Mom and Dad	$1,200.00	$0.00	$0.00	$1,200.00	$0.00	$2,400.00
Work	$1,100.00	$1,100.00	$1,100.00	$1,100.00	$1,100.00	$5,500.00
Monthly Income	$2,300.00	$1,100.00	$1,100.00	$2,300.00	$1,100.00	
Shape In, Monthly	$10.00	$15.00	$135.00	$30.00	$135.00	

FIGURE 4.6 *Expenses versus Income, January through May*

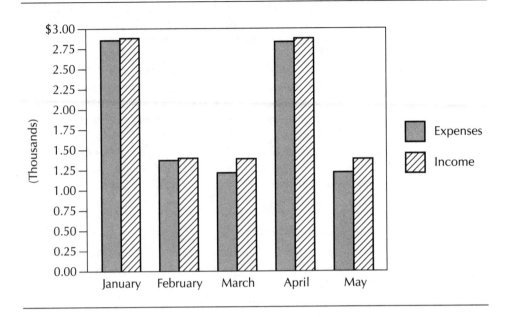

FIGURE 4.7 *Renet's Expenses, Month of January*

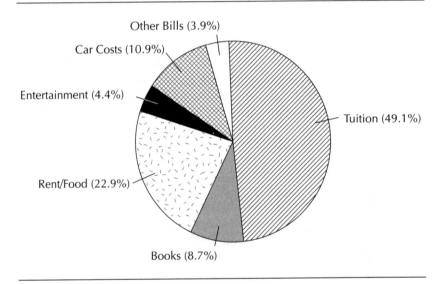

include spreadsheets. An excellent spreadsheet for beginners and students is *The Cruncher* (IBM and IBM compatibles with Windows and Macintosh computers) by Davidson. It has easy-to-use instructions and plenty of examples.

The activity in Try This 4.5 was designed to help you learn a spreadsheet program. If you do not have access to an integrated package or a spreadsheet program, you may wish to skip this activity.

> **Try This 4.5** *Have your students use a spreadsheet package and create a budget (you provide the raw data), similar to the budget shown in Figure 4.5. Their budget should include all an-*

*ticipated sources of income and all anticipated expenses. In ad-
dition, have the students choose one month and create a bar
graph and a pie chart, both with labels, showing the expenses.
Examples of these two types of graphs are shown In Figures 4.6
and 4.7.*

The activity in Try This 4.6 shows students that spreadsheets and word-
processing packages can be used together to present information.

> ***Try This 4.6*** *Have your students use a word-processing pack-
> age to write a letter to their parents or a friend, asking for an in-
> crease in their income. Have them include and refer to their bud-
> get and charts done in Try This 4.5.*

Conclusion

If students can use a few of the software packages mentioned in this chapter,
they will be more prepared for the workplace. Most colleges and universities
teach students these software packages in their Introduction to Computing
course. We would like to reemphasize that the students should be taught only
the basics. Some of these software packages are very complex and confusing.
By sticking to the basics, students will quickly get good results and will develop a solid foundation for learning the more complex parts of the software
at a later time.

The following list includes several additional points we believe are important to consider when using computers.

Helpful Hints for Computer Use

1. Use computers in all of the methods listed in this chapter.
2. Use computers to prepare the students for life after school.
3. Have the students use computers enough so that they are comfortable
   with them.
4. Use CAI as a way to give students more self-confidence and generate
   positive attitudes toward learning.
5. Teach students that computers are a tool to help them overcome their
   disabilities.
6. Use computers as a tool to teach new material to students.
7. Choose the software based on needs of the students and the curriculum. Do not modify the curriculum to fit the CAI available.
8. Carefully consider placement of the computers in the classroom.
9. Devise and display a computer time schedule in the class.
10. Take advantage of the many aspects of computers, such as graphics
    and sound, to motivate the students and to keep their attention.
11. Customize software where possible to have it meet the needs of the
    students.
12. Select software based on the academic levels of the students, the spe-
    cial learning characteristics of the students, and the skills that the
    students need to learn.
13. Show students practical applications of the computer in their school-
    work and life.
14. Use computers yourself to monitor students' performances and to
    make your job easier.

References

Bitter, G. G., Camuse, R. A., & Durbin, V. L. (1993). *Using a Microcomputer in the Classroom* (3rd ed.). Boston: Allyn and Bacon.

Bottage, B. A., & Hasselbring, T. S. (1993). A Comparison of Two Approaches for Teaching Complex, Authentic Mathematics Problems to Adolescents in Remedial Math Classes. *Exceptional Children*, 59(6), 556–566.

Duke, P., & Rumpp. G. (1994, November 18). *"Decisions, Decisions": Cooperative Technology Learning Groups.* Paper presented at the annual meeting of the National Council of States Inservice Educators (NCSIE), Charleston, SC. (November 18).

Frankel, S. (1990). Write right. *The Sunday Oregonian*, May 27, pp. K1, B4.

Gardner, J. E., Taber-Brown, F. M., & Wissick, C. A. (1992). Selecting Age-Appropriate Software for Adolescents and Adults with Developmental Disabilities. *Teaching Exceptional Children*, 24(3), 60–63.

Lewis, R. B., (1993). *Special Education Technology: Classroom Applications*. Pacific Grove, CA: Brooks/Cole Publishing.

Littauer, J. (1994). A "How To . . ." on Using Courseware in the Classroom. *Technological Horizons in Education Journal*, 22(1), 53–54.

Lubke, M. M., Rogers, B., & Evans, K. T. (1989). Teaching Fractions with Videodiscs. *Teaching Exceptional Children*, 21(3), 55–56.

Malouf, D. B., Jamison, P. J., Kercher, M. H., & Carlucci, C. M. (1991). Computer Software Aids Effective Instruction. *Teaching Exceptional Children*, 23(2), 56–57.

Malouf, D. B., Jamison, P. J., Kercher, M. H., & Carlucci, C. M. (1991). Integrating Computer Software into Effective Instruction. *Teaching Exceptional Children*, 23(3), 54–56.

Malouf, D. B., Jamison, P. J., Kercher, M. H., & Carlucci, C. M. (1991). Integrating Computer Software into Effective Instruction (Part 2). *Teaching Exceptional Children*, 23(4), 57–60.

Montague, M., & Fonseca, F. (1993). Using Computers to Improve Story Writing. *Teaching Exceptional Children*, 25(4), 46–60.

Perry, M., & Garber, M. (1993). Technology helps parents teach their children with developmental delays. *Teaching Exceptional Children*, 25(2), 8–11.

Raskind, M. (1993). Assistive Technology and Adults with Learning Disabilities: A Blueprint for Exploration and Advancement. *Learning Disabilities Quarterly*, 16, 185–196.

van Daal, V. H. P., & van der Leij, A. (1992). Computer Based Reading and Spelling Practice for Children with Learning Disabilities. *Journal of Learning Disabilities*, 25, 186–195.

Vockell, E. L., & Mihail, T. (1993). Principles Behind Computerized Instruction for Students with Exceptionalities. *Teaching Exceptional Children*, 25(3), 39–43.

Woodward, J., & Howard, L. (1994). The Misconceptions of Youth: Errors and Their Mathematical Meaning. *Exceptional Children*, 61(2), 126–136.

5

Computer-Managed Instruction

Gary Ross
William N. Bender

*U*pon completion of this chapter you should be able to:

◆ *Identify CMI software for classroom management tools.*

◆ *Identify software for individualized education plans.*

◆ *Identify software for behavior support.*

Computers are tools that can be used not only to assist students as they learn but also to help with classroom management. Classroom management includes daily activities—such as keeping track of attendance, grades, and student performance—and periodic activities—such as letters and notes to parents, report cards, materials requests, inventory, and individualized education plans (IEPs). These activities generally fall under the category of computer-managed instruction (CMI).

During the early years of computer use in the classroom, there was great promise of software that would turn the computer into an all-purpose management tool that would track classroom essentials such as taking attendance, monitoring behavior, generating IEP goals and objectives, and overseeing student progress. Some of these promises have been met at various times throughout the short history of computer use in the classroom. For example, *AIMSTAR: Charting and Graphing Individualized Student Data in the Classroom* was an early attempt to provide a way to visually analyze student data and to provide program choices for the teacher. As data were collected during training/observation periods and entered into the computer, the computer would generate a graphic display of the data and, depending on previously entered goals, give the teacher feedback as to whether the student's program was on track or needed adjustment to reach the aim.

In spite of this early attempt, computer-based management for classroom teachers is a promise that has remained largely unfulfilled. To date, an all-purpose management package that will meet the overall needs of teachers has not been developed. Currently, there are software packages that will meet the needs of teachers in *specific areas* of classroom management, but there is not an all-encompassing CMI package available. Therefore, the software packages for classroom management discussed in this chapter will address specific needs within the overall management picture. The CMI options presented include monitoring attendance rolls, gradebooks, and student progress; generating classroom materials, report cards, letters to parents, and IEPs; and collecting, managing, and analyzing data for behavior support.

The sections of this chapter may be used as individual segments or combined in any manner that meets your needs. Each segment is intended to require about an hour of interaction time. Some of the CMI options discussed here are software packages, whereas other options utilize existing computer utility software such as word-processing, spreadsheet, or database programs.

Classroom Management Tools

Classroom management tools include those programs that assist in the maintenance of information concerning attendance, grades, schedules, lesson plans, communications, and materials generation. These functions are often repetitive, and therefore are enhanced and made easier through the use of a computer. This section will examine the use of a computer in fulfilling each of these functions. There are a few software packages that provide programs to facilitate each of these functions; however, some of the programs are not user friendly and other programs are expensive.

Many CMI options are available to teachers who have access to a "works" program such as *AppleWorks*, *Microsoft Works*, or *Claris Works*. (An address for each of these programs may be found in Appendix II.) These programs each contain word-processing, database, and spreadsheet programs, and the components of each of these programs can interact with each other. That is, each "works" program allows for the easy transfer of data from one function to another. For example, an attendance roll can be developed and the data then transferred to a gradebook or other documents.

Although the most common computer in the school is probably the Macintosh series, some schools do have IBM and IBM compatible computers with *Windows*. Of the three "works" packages mentioned in the preceding paragraph, *AppleWorks* is the only one that will run on an Apple II computer. *Microsoft Works* and *Claris Works* are available for both Macintosh, IBM, and IBM-compatible computers. Furthermore, both *Microsoft Works* and *Claris Works* allow teachers to use data from programs in *AppleWorks*. In our opinion, *Claris Works* offers the best value, a blend of price, ease of use, and features in a CMI program. Therefore, the activities and options for the classroom management functions discussed here will be illustrated using *Claris Works*.

In addition to the "works" programs previously mentioned, there are programs that are specifically designed for teachers to use for grading and attendance. For example, *Grade 2* (available for Macintosh computers, and IBM and IBM compatible computers with and without *Windows*) by Excelsior Software, Inc., is a CMI program for teachers to help with attendance, grades, and report generation, to name just a few. Since it was designed for teachers, it is easy to use and includes useful examples of classroom management documents. These documents can be modified for specific classrooms. Thus, in some instances, teachers do not have to create the entire document.

Unlike some of the other chapters of this text, this chapter includes specific instructions for using a specific computer package. We believe that the "mechanics" of CMI make these specific examples necessary and desirable. It is important to remember that the process of developing these CMI options in any of the previously mentioned packages is similar. That is, the functions, features, and commands are enough alike in all of these packages that once a teacher has mastered the development of an option in one package, he or she should be able to accomplish it in any of the two other packages. For this reason, highly specific instructions for computer setup of various programs are included in Figures 5.2, 5.4, and 5.10 in this chapter.

We present several "templates" for these CMI tasks. Think of each template as a blank form that you may wish to save. Later, when you want to work on a particular class management function, you load the template (or bring the form up on the screen) and save a copy of the template under the name of the working program. This copy then becomes the working program; the original template will be saved on the disk for future use. For example, if you want to write a letter to parents about Special Olympics, you should load the parents' "Letter Template," save a copy as "Special Olympics Letter," and then make the changes desired before printing and sending it home with the students. That way, you do not have to create these letter templates over and over. We will now discuss how to develop templates for some of the activities involved in classroom management.

Attendance Rolls

Daily attendance is usually collected by the office, and records are kept there and distributed to the teachers as needed. However, it may be desirable to record attendance in individual classes and at activities. This section will provide instruction on the setup, development, and management of attendance rolls using a spreadsheet program.

The activity in Try This 5.1 is designed to guide you through the creation of a computerized attendance roll. If you already have one, you may wish to skip this activity.

> ***Try This 5.1*** *Develop an Attendance Roll using the steps described below. Use Figure 5.1 as a model. Figure 5.2 gives specific instructions for use with* Claris Works.

The basic idea is the following. First, create a template and save it. Then copy the template and use the copy for the actual roll. Once the template is created, you only have to copy it and save it under another name to create several months of attendance rolls. You do not have to create each separate roll.

Now we will consider the template in more detail. On the attendance roll in Figure 5.1, we use 11 columns. The first item of business is to determine the number of rows and columns. Second, adjust the width of the columns taking into account the information that they will contain. Third, enter column headings. Finally, enter your data. Specific instructions for this procedure using *Claris Works* are given in Figure 5.2.

You now have a template for attendance rolls. To make copies to use in the classroom, open the template and "save as" using a unique name for each roll. Then make the changes to the date and student names and save again.

Gradebook

Almost all teachers must keep track of grades on various activities during the marking period. To facilitate the recording of grades, this section will provide instruction on the setup, development, and management of a gradebook using

FIGURE 5.1   Attendance: Ms. Smith, Class 95/96

1				************ 1st Quarter ************						
2	**Week 1**			**Days**						
3	**Students**	Mon	Tue	Wed	Thur	Fri	Present	Absent	P to D	A to D
4	Student 1	1	1	1	1	0	4	1	4	1
5	Student 2	1	1	1	1	1	5	0	5	0
6	Student 3	1	1	1	1	1	5	0	5	0
7	Student 4	1	0	0	0	1	2	3	2	3
8	Student 5	1	1	1	1	1	5	0	5	0
9	Student 6	1	1	1	1	1	5	0	5	0
10	Student 7	1	0	1	0	1	3	2	3	2
11	Student 8	1	1	1	1	1	5	0	5	0
12	Student 9	1	1	1	1	1	5	0	5	0
13	Student 10	1	1	1	1	1	5	0	5	0
14	Student 11	1	1	1	1	1	5	0	5	0
15	Student 12	1	0	1	0	0	2	3	2	3
16	Student 13	1	1	1	1	1	5	0	5	0
17	Student 14	1	1	1	1	1	5	0	5	0
18										
19	**Week 2**			**Days**						
20	**Students**	Mon	Tue	Wed	Thur	Fri	Present	Absent	P to D	A to D
21	Student 1	1	1	1	1	0	4	1	8	2
22	Student 2	1	1	1	1	1	5	0	10	0
23	Student 3	1	1	1	1	1	5	0	10	0
24	Student 4	1	0	0	0	1	2	3	4	6
25	Student 5	1	1	1	1	1	5	0	10	0
26	Student 6	1	1	1	1	1	5	0	10	0
27	Student 7	1	0	1	0	1	3	2	6	4
28	Student 8	1	1	1	1	1	5	0	10	0
29	Student 9	1	1	1	1	1	5	0	10	0
30	Student 10	1	1	1	1	1	5	0	10	0
31	Student 11	1	1	1	1	1	5	0	10	0
32	Student 12	1	0	1	0	0	2	3	4	6
33	Student 13	1	1	1	1	1	5	0	10	0
34	Student 14	1	1	1	1	1	5	0	10	0
35										
36	**Week 3**			**Days**						
37	**Students**	Mon	Tue	Wed	Thur	Fri	Present	Absent	P to D	A to D
38	Student 1	1	1	1	1	0	4	1	12	3
39	Student 2	1	1	1	1	1	5	0	15	0
40	Student 3	1	1	1	1	1	5	0	15	0
41	Student 4	1	0	0	0	1	2	3	6	9
42	Student 5	1	1	1	1	1	5	0	15	0
43	Student 6	1	1	1	1	1	5	0	15	0
44	Student 7	1	0	1	0	1	3	2	9	6
45	Student 8	1	1	1	1	1	5	0	15	0
46	Student 9	1	1	1	1	1	5	0	15	0
47	Student 10	1	1	1	1	1	5	0	15	0
48	Student 11	1	1	1	1	1	5	0	15	0
49	Student 12	1	0	1	0	0	2	3	6	9

FIGURE 5.2 **Claris Works** *Instructions for an Attendance Roll*

1. Open *Claris Works* and click on the spreadsheet.
2. Save the spreadsheet as "Attendance Template."
3. Format the spreadsheet under the Format menu to contain 10 columns and 619 rows.
4. Set the column widths as follows:
   Column A to 72;
   B, C, D, E, F, G, H, I, J to 40.
5. Insert a heading centered over the spreadsheet using the tab key: "Attendance: (teacher name) Class 95/96."
6. Type "**********1st Quarter**********" in cell C1;
   "Week 1" in cell A2;
   "Days" in D2;
   "Students" in cell A3;
   the days of the week in cells B3 through F3;
   "Present" in cell G3;
   "Absent" in H3;
   "P to D" (presents to date) in I3;
   "A to D" (absences to date) in J3.
   This takes care of the column headings for Week 1.
7. In cells A4 through say A18, for as many students as you have, enter the names of your students. Note, if you have more than 15 students, you will have to increase the number of rows formatted to be like the rest of the template.
8. Now you need to create the templates for the other eight weeks.
   a. Select cells A2 through J18 (this number will be the number of students you have) by dragging the cursor, using the mouse, diagonally down across these cells and then copy them.

      Week 2. Select cells A19 through J35 and paste the copies cells into them.
      Week 3. Select cells A36 through J52 and paste the copies cells into them.
      Week 4. Select cells A53 through J69 and paste the copies cells into them.
      Week 5. Select cells A70 through J86 and paste the copies cells into them.
      Week 6. Select cells A87 through J103 and paste the copies cells into them.
      Week 7. Select cells A104 through J120 and paste the copies cells into them.
      Week 8. Select cells A121 through J137 and paste the copies cells into them.
      Week 9. Select cells A138 through J154 and paste the copies cells into them.
9. Create the templates for the other three quarters.
   a. Select cells A1 through J154 and copy them.
   b. Select cell A156 and do a paste (this takes care of the second quarter).
   Select cell A311 and do a paste (this takes care of the third quarter).
   Select cell A466 and do a paste (this takes care of the fourth quarter).
10. Now you need to install the function that will calculate the total times each students has attended.
    a. For the times present during the week (the Present column first:
       i. Select cell G3 and paste the function "Count2" into it.
       ii. Modify the pasted function by typing "1,B4..F4" inside the parentheses then press Return.
       iii. Select cell G4 and then the column head "G." This will select all the cells in this column. Go to the Calculate menu and select "Fill Down." This will put the formula in all those cells with correct references to cells.
    b. For the times absent during the week (the Absent column) first:
       i. Select cell G4 and do a copy.
       ii. Select cell H4 and do a paste.

continued

FIGURE 5.2 **Continued**

---

    iii. Select cell H4 and then the column head "H." This will select all the cells in this column. Go to the Calculate menu and select "Fill Down." This will put the formula in all those cells with correct references to cells.

  c. The formulas for times present and absent to date are a little more complicated.

    i. Select cell I4, type "=SUM(G4)" and press Return.

    ii. Select cell I4 and then drag down through cells I4 to I17. This will select these cells in column I. Go to the Calculate menu and select "Fill Down." This will put the formula in all those cells with correct references to cells.

    iii. Select cell I4, do a copy, select cell J4 and do a paste and press Return.

    iv. Select cell J4 and then drag down through cells J4 to J17. This will select these cells in column J. Go to the Calculate menu and select "Fill Down." This will put the formula in all those cells with correct references to cells.

    v. To put present and absent formulas in subsequent weeks, you need to repeat steps 3 and 4, but select the cell for student 1 in column I for the prior week instead of cell I4.

    vi. After you have selected this cell and copied it, select the cell for student 1 in column I for the new week and do a paste. It is now necessary to insert "G4+" between the opening parenthesis and the first "G" and press Return. You will have to insert "G4+" for each new week as you paste the formula from the previous week.

    vii. Now select the cells in column I for the new week. This will select the needed cells in column I. Go to the Calculate menu and select "Fill Down." This will put the formula in all those cells with correct references to cells.

    viii. Now select the cell for student 1 in column J for the new week, do a paste, press Return, and drag down through cells in column J for the new week. This will select the needed cells in column J. Go to the Calculate menu and select "Fill Down." This will put the formula in all those cells with correct references to cells.

    ix. Repeat steps 5 through 8 for each subsequent week, remembering to go to the first cell in column I for the previous week to copy the formula and to insert "G4+" into the formula after the paste.

---

a spreadsheet program. Collecting, analyzing, and reporting data on student behavioral performance are important elements of data-based teaching. These elements will be covered in detail in the section on Behavior Support.

    The activity in Try This 5.2 is designed to guide you through the creation of a gradebook. The instructions are similar to the attendance roll. If you created a computerized attendance roll or already have a computerized gradebook, you may wish to skip this activity.

> ***Try This 5.2***   *Develop a Gradebook using a spreadsheet program and the steps described below. You may use Figure 5.3 as a guide. The instructions for the gradebook in Figure 5.3 using the program Claris Works are found in Figure 5.4.*

    By following Try This 5.2, you now have a template for a gradebook. Remember always to save any changes.

Report Card

Report cards that use the standard form required by the school district may be less than adequate for evaluating the needs and progress of students with disabilities or students who are at-risk. Thus, many teachers develop some type of additional "report card" for use with these students. In addition to the required report card, an anecdotal report will convey a more meaningful appraisal of the student's performance. Anecdotal reports may also be better

FIGURE 5.3   Gradebook: English Period 2

Assignment	1	2	3	4	5	6	7	8	9	10	11	12	13	14	15	16	17	18	19	20	21	22	23	24	25	26	Average	Extra	Final
Students																													
Student 1	80	76	100																								85.333	5	90
Student 2	76	87	74																								79	6	85
Student 3	89	83	85																								85.666	4	90
Student 4	67	74	90																								77	2	79
Student 5	57	76	82																								71.666	1	73
Student 6	90	85	91																								88.666	4	93
Student 7	89	89	82																								86.666	5	92
Student 8	87	81	78																								82	3	85
Student 9	79	80	88																								82.333	4	86
Student 10	93	84	83																								86.666	5	92
Student 11	90	85	84																								86.333	6	92
Student 12	75	80	85																								80	8	88
Student 13	78	77	80																								78.333	4	82
Student 14	76	73	78																								75.666	3	79

Assign 1	Write personal info
Assign 2	Fill in personal info on job app
Assign 3	Write education
Assign 4	Fill in education on job app
Assign 5	
Assign 6	
Assign 7	
Assign 8	
Assign 9	
Assign 10	
Assign 11	
Assign 12	
Assign 13	
Assign 14	
Assign 15	
Assign 16	
Assign 17	
Assign 18	
Assign 19	
Assign 20	
Assign 21	
Assign 22	
Assign 23	
Assign 24	
Assign 25	
Assign 26	

FIGURE 5.4 ***Gradebook Instructions for* Claris Works**

1. Open *Claris Works* and click the mouse on the spreadsheet.
2. Save the spreadsheet as "Gradebook Template."
3. Format the spreadsheet under the Format menu to contain 30 columns and 46 rows.
4. Set the column widths as follows:
   Columns A to 60;
   B-AA to 20;
   AB to 34;
   AC & AD to 30.
5. Set the row height to 11 for all rows.
6. Set the default font to "Times" size 9.
7. Insert the heading centered over the spreadsheet with tab "Gradebook: (subject) (period)" (see Figure 5.3).
8. Enter "Assignment" in cell A1,
   "Students" in cell A2,
   the number of the assignment in cells B1 through AA1,
   "Average" in cell AB1,
   "Extra" in AC1,
   Final in AD1 (see Figure 5.3).
   This sets up the column headings for the gradebook.
9. In cells A3 through A15, for as many students as you have, enter the names of your students. Note, if you have more than 14 students, you will have to increase the number of rows.
10. Now you need to enter the function that will average the grades for you.
    a. Select cell AB3.
    b. Paste the function "Average" into cell AB3. Highlight the cell range in the function and drag the cursor across cells B3 to AA3. The function should now look like this: =AVERAGE(B3..AA3). Press Return.
    c. Select cell AB3 and do a copy from the "Edit" menu.
    d. Press the down arrow. Cell AB4 will be highlighted. Do a paste. Continue in this manner until the cells in column AB that have students contain the function. That is, select the cell with the down arrow and do a paste. *Claris Works* will automatically adjust the cells used in the computation of the average for each student.
11. The following steps explain how to install the function to calculate the final grade for each student.
    a. Select cell AD3 and paste the function "Round" into it.
    b. Modify the pasted function by typing the following inside the parentheses: AB3+AC3,0. This function adds the average and extra points and rounds the result to give an integer grade. On your screen it should look like =ROUND(AB3+AC3,0). After finishing this, press Return.
    c. Select cell AD3 and do a copy from the "edit" menu. Press the down arrow and cell AD4 will be highlighted. Do a paste from the "Edit" menu and press the down arrow to put the function in cell AD4. Continue, in this manner, to paste the function into all the cells in the "Final" column for all students.
12. Since there is excess space on the page, it would be good to enter a brief description of each assignment. This can be achieved by the following steps.
    a. Since there are 26 assignments in this template, we can create two columns of 13 assignments each. Select cell A34 and type Assign 1 into it.
    b. Continue selecting the remaining cells in column A and enter Assign 2 to 13.
    c. Select cell O34 and enter Assign 14 into it. The text will automatically consume as many cells as needed. Continue selecting the remaining cells in column O and enter Assign 15 to 26.
    d. To enter the description for an assignment select the adjacent cell and type in the description. Figure 5.3 shows an example of this.

suited to describing student performance on specific IEP objectives. Once a template for this task is created, the creation of anecdotal reports should not be a time-consuming task.

The activity in Try This 5.3 is designed to make your workload a bit lighter by creating a report card using a word-processing package. If you have already done this, you may wish to skip this activity.

> ***Try This 5.3*** *Develop a Report Card. You can use Figure 5.5 as a guide. This example was done using a word-processing package.*

FIGURE 5.5 Quarterly Review

Dear Mr. and Mrs. Jamison:

This is our review on Jacob's progress. As was explained in our meeting, I will be sending this review home with the traditional Report Card because I believe there is often more to consider when reviewing Jacob's progress than can be communicated on the Report Card. First, let me say that it continues to be a pleasure to have Jacob in my class. He has such potential and has been trying hard to accomplish the goals set out for him. We appreciate all you have done to reinforce his training at home. Overall, Jacob has remained consistent in his progress. I have broken the review down according to the goal areas we outlined on his IEP. You received a copy of those goals at the IEP meeting.

Jacob continues to improve his reading skills. He has mastered recognition of survival words related to gender, thanks in great part to the practice you have been giving him at home and on trips. He has improved in recognizing the words related to safety and health also. However, mastery goals have not been met, so we will continue to work on these next quarter. The words we will work on are *exit, enter, danger, poison, keep out, hospital, walk,* and *don't walk.* If you could continue to practice with these words whenever you see them, it will increase Jacob's ability to spot them in different settings. Likewise, reading the shopping list is going well. We will continue with the words we have been using and add: *dish detergent, napkins, tuna fish, Spam, Cheerios,* and *orange juice.*

I hope you have noticed the great improvement Jacob has made using the "Dollar Plus" system. He has really caught on to this and it has made shopping much more relaxed for him. He has told us how you let him pay for things at the store and this is good for him. With this skill, as with all others, it is important that Jacob be able to practice in as many settings as possible and to continue to practice from time to time. If the practice is not continued, the skill will be lost. This is why we are so happy that you are able to work with Jacob.

The work we are doing in vocational skills is more difficult for Jacob and will take longer, but he is making progress. He seems to have the most trouble remembering what to do in various situations such as clocking in when he gets to the job. Overall, we see improvement and are trying to reinforce his use of the cue cards that we sent home. If you can practice with him, it would really help.

Jacob is a lucky young man to have parents who are willing to help him to such an extent. As I told you before, he can learn these skills; it is just going to take a little longer. Again, thanks for your help and let us know if you have any questions or suggestions.

Yours,

Renet Lovorn, M.Ed.

The development of an anecdotal report card will not be a complex task if you have completed the task sequences for developing an attendance roll and a gradebook described earlier in the chapter. Of course, practice on these tasks will allow you to become much more fluent in development of these CMI options for your class.

Letters to Parents

Correspondence to parents and others about classroom activities or student performance is easier than ever when using the computer. Letters and notices can be personalized by making a template and changing the names for each student. The busy teacher who wants to share classroom activities and keep parents informed between report card dates will find this option very useful. Teachers can significantly enhance their communication with parents by creation of a "parent letter" template and frequent use of it. Some teachers set a goal for themselves of sending at least five parent letters home each week. Remember to send positive and complimentary letters home at least as often as you send "problem" letters home. This guideline will make your relationships with students' parents go much more smoothly. Figure 5.6 is an example of such a letter.

IEP Generation

Individualized education plans (IEPs) are required by law for all special education students. The generation and annual review processes to develop and review IEPs require a great deal of time and effort. When a computer is used in this process, the time and effort required can be reduced considerably, and this results in less paperwork for teachers.

However, one unfortunate result of the use of computer-generated IEP packages is the reduction in true "individualization" of the IEP. In other words, the IEPs for all students with disabilities tend to look alike when using these programs. This reduction in individualization is due to the way many of the early computerized IEP-generation programs work. When computerization of the IEP-generation process is attempted, in some cases, the first

FIGURE 5.6 Parent Letter

May 5

Dear Mr. and Mrs. Clay:

Your son Tony has an opportunity to participate in the Special Olympics. As you know, this competition was designed for students with disabilities, much like Tony.

The Olympics will be held at Okey High School on Highway 33, and will start at 9:00 A.M. on Saturday May 17. Tony is extremely excited about the competition and we hope that he will be able to participate.

If you have any questions, please contact me. We hope to see you there.

Sincerely,

Ms. Renet Lovorn

thing considered are the attributes of the computer that facilitate storage and retrieval of large amounts of information. Using a computer, a teacher can retrieve objectives from a large computer database to create the IEP. Thus, he or she has access to a tremendous time-saving tool. This process is much easier than creating an IEP by hand. However, in some of the available programs, the objectives have to be taken as they exist in the database, with little or no editing. This tends to create a more uniform product, and the individualization of the objectives for the IEP may be compromised.

There are several programs that facilitate the generation of IEPs in an efficient manner with little loss of individualization. When used to create IEPs that sustain the "spirit of individualization," these programs can increase the effectiveness of the teacher and save considerable time in IEP generation.

The SEMS Program

Special Education Management System (SEMS) is a CMI program for development of computerized IEPs. This package is commercially available from Eutactics, Inc., and is available for Macintosh computers, and IBM and IBM compatible computers with and without *Windows*. When *SEMS* is purchased, Eutactics will work with local school districts or states to meet state requirements for individualized reports. For example, the state of Georgia has purchased the *SEMS* package and the package has been modified specifically for reports utilized in Georgia.

SEMS produces IEPs from over 10,000 goals and objectives, but is much more than an IEP program. It also produces federal and state reports, student reports, and service/exceptionality reports. Thus, it is a great assistance in the administrative headcounting required in special education.

Within the "present levels of performance" section, the user may enter the data directly from other test protocols and observation notes or he or she may select from a prepackaged series of statements developed for each exceptionality at each level. The user selects goals then objectives. After an appropriate objective is chosen, the modifiers for that objective are selected. The user may modify the objectives by selecting the criterion by which the objective will be measured, the conditions for the performance of the objective, and the methods used for evaluation.

Users may add options to the database that will thereafter appear during IEP entry. Standard sentences and phrases may be added that will then remain in the database and may be selected later for other students. The program also offers the flexibility so that a user may add (merely by typing in) a sentence to a student's IEP. Also, any of the standard sentences in the database may be edited within a particular student's IEP. This flexibility offers the option of totally individualized IEP preparation coupled with an extensive system that can generate the required special education administration report data.

At any point, within the context of IEP development, a user may select the "IEP minutes" option, which presents a word processor on the screen. The user may then type in any notes that he or she wishes to save. This function can save up to a page of notes for each IEP. These are not reproduced on the IEP but are saved as notes for the meeting.

Finally, *SEMS* offers an extensive on-line help system such that from any screen, the user may request assistance and then return to the task. The system is also supported by a 1–800 phone number for access to the developers.

Bonanza! and *Goal Rush*

Bonanza! and *Goal Rush* are two IEP packages from IEP, Inc. *Bonanza!* is similar to *SEMS* in that it is customized for individual states, school districts, and schools. There are versions of *Bonanza!* for IBM, IBM-compatible, and Macintosh computers. These include over 5,000 goals and objectives. In addition, there is a smaller version (2,000 goals and objectives) that will run on Apple IIe computers.

Goal Rush is a computerized IEP package that can be purchased with a districtwide license or an individual user license. The program comes with a library of goals and objectives on disk called "Goal Mine." New goals and objectives can easily be added as needed. Furthermore, when you purchase *Goal Rush*, the company will modify the program to generate your district's IEP forms. There are versions of *Goal Rush* for IBM, IBM-compatible, and Macintosh computers.

Goal Rush is an easy-to-use, menu-driven program. In addition to the selection of goals, objectives, criterions, and methods, *Goal Rush* allows the teacher to insert easily his or her own text for a special situation. Furthermore, goals and objectives can be added to the library using the menu selection.

Goal Rush is not as sophisticated as the program discussed earlier and does not offer as many choices. However, it does give a high-quality product and the price can be easily afforded by most schools. The company has indicated a willingness and desire to work with individual teachers, schools, and school districts. Figure 5.7 presents a portion of an IEP generated by *Goal Rush*.

Cautions on Computer-Generated IEPs

It is important to remember that this tool, like any other tool, can be abused. Two precautions are worth noting. First, it is tempting to continue year after year with the same basic IEP. Obviously, teachers should consider each student's individual needs each year and not abrogate the responsibility of developing an effective individual IEP on a yearly basis. Second, it is possible to develop the entire IEP before the official meeting and thereby at least give the appearance that the parents' input is not important. This situation can be minimized by having the computer available at the time of the meeting, making requested changes, and printing out the completed IEP for signatures.

Overall, the computer generation of IEPs promises to save teachers considerable time, and, in many ways, computer-generated IEPs can lead to more individualized IEPs. However, the foregoing precautions should be kept in mind.

Behavior Support

Behavior support includes collecting, managing, and analyzing data on student behavior. The behaviors may be of an academic, social, or functional nature. The procedures for all of these are similar. That is, it does not matter whether the behavior being observed is two-digit addition with regrouping, getting to class on time, or brushing teeth. The data on performance still need to be collected, managed, analyzed, and reported. The tools, data sheets, graphs, and reports used for the different behaviors may look different or contain different elements, but having mastered the creation of one style of tool, the teacher will be able to create tools for all types of behavior.

FIGURE 5.7   Goal Rush IEP

<Name of licensee appears here: district or person & title>
Individual Education Plan
Francis X. Murray

===
GOAL: DEVELOP PRE-KINDERGARTEN COMMUNICATION SKILLS
===

OBJECTIVE	CRITERION	BEGIN
=========	=========	=========
Raise arms when parent (or caregiver) says, "Come here" or "Up" while reaching toward child.	increase by 40%	_____
Nod head for "yes," indicating the understanding of a simple question.	when requested	_____
Shake head "no" at the appropriate time to indicate comprehension.	in 5 out of 10 trials	_____
Wave "bye-bye" at the appropriate time to indicate comprehension.	3 times out of 4	_____
Show a facial response to the ringing of a bell or other sudden noise.	50% of the time	_____
Say "mama" or "dada" or other family names with purpose and meaning.	when requested	_____
Use jabbering as if talking, although sounds are unintelligible to adults.	for 5 seconds	_____
Vocalize to a toy or pet.	each day	_____
Make "singing" tones.	when requested	_____
Imitate sounds or words of others.	in 5 out of 10 trials	_____

These tools may be developed using a "works" program. The programs have sufficient capabilities for creating behavior support tools for classroom use. The examples here use *Claris Works.*

Collecting and Managing Data

The activity in Try This 5.4 is designed to help you think about managing student data. Depending on the type of students you teach, you may wish to skip this activity.

> ***Try This 5.4***   *Develop data collection and data management sheets using a word-processing program and the steps below. You*

may wish to use Figures 5.8 and 5.9 as guides. The instructions for creating these sheets using Claris Works *can be found in Figure 5.10.*

First, create a template; save it and then copy it. You will use the copy for your actual data sheets. Once the template is created, you only have to copy it and save it under another name to create several different data sheets.

FIGURE 5.8   *Data Sheet: Time-Delay, Sight Words*

Student _____   Teacher _____

#	A	B	C	D	E	F	G	H	I	J	K	L	M	N	O	P	Q	R	S
1	Date					Date					Date					Date			
2	Session					Session					Session					Session			
3	Start Time					Start Time					Start Time					Start Time			
4	Stop Time					Stop Time					Stop Time					Stop Time			
5	Total Time					Total Time					Total Time					Total Time			
6	Delay					Delay					Delay					Delay			
7	Trial	Word	B/4	Aft		Trial	Word	B/4	Aft		Trial	Word	B/4	Aft		Trial	Word	B/4	Aft
8																			
9	1			1		1		2			1			1		1		1	
10	2			2		2		2			2		1			2		1	
11	3			1		3		1			3			1		3		1	
12	4			2		4			2		4		2			4			1
13	5			2		5		1			5		1			5		1	
14	6			0		6		2			6		2			6		1	
15	7			0		7			1		7		1			7		1	
16	8			1		8		1			8		1			8		1	
17	9			1		9			1		9		1			9		1	
18	10		1			10		1			10		1			10		1	
19	11		1			11		1			11		1			11		1	
20	12		2			12		2			12		2			12		2	
21	13		1			13		1			13		1			13		1	
22	14		1			14		1			14		1			14		1	
23	15			1		15			1		15			1		15		1	
24	16		1			16		1			16		1			16		1	
25	17		2			17		2			17		2			17		2	
26	18		1			18		1			18		1			18		1	
27	19		1			19		1			19		1			19		1	
28	20		1			20		1			20		1			20		1	
29	Column Total		10	10				16	4				17	3				19	1
30	# Correct		8	5		# Correct		11	3		# Correct		13	3		# Correct		17	1
31	% Correct		40%	25%		% Correct		55%	15%		% Correct		65%	15%		% Correct		85%	5%
32	# Incorrect		2	3		# Incorrect		5	1		# Incorrect		4	0		# Incorrect		2	0
33	% Incorrect		10%	15%		% Incorrect		25%	5%		% Incorrect		20%	0%		% Incorrect		10%	0%
34	# No Response		0	2		# No Response		0	0		# No Response		0	0		# No Response		0	0
35	% No Response		0%	10%		% No Response		0%	0%		% No Response		0%	0%		% No Response		0%	0%
36																			
37	Total # Correct/B4			49		Total # No Resp/B4			0							Total # Incorrect/Aft		4	
38	Total % Correct/B4			61%		Total % No Resp/B4			0%							Total % Incorrect/Aft		5%	
39	Total # Incorrect/B4			13		Total # Correct/Aft			39							Total # No Resp/Aft		2	
40	Total % Incorrect/B4			65%		Total % Correct/Aft			49%							Total % No Resp/Aft		2%	

Key = + = Correct
− = Incorrect
0 = No Response

FIGURE 5.9 Data Management: Time-Delay, Sight Words

Student _____   Teacher _____

	A	B	C	D	E	F	G	H	I	J	K	L	M	N	O	P	Q	R	S
1	Date					Date					Date					Date			
2	Session 1					Session 2					Session 3					Session 4			
3	Start Time					Start Time					Start Time					Start Time			
4	Stop Time					Stop Time					Stop Time					Stop Time			
5	Total Time					Total Time					Total Time					Total Time			
6	Delay					Delay					Delay					Delay			
7	Trial	Word	B/4	Aft		Trial	Word	B/4	Aft		Trial	Word	B/4	Aft		Trial	Word	B/4	Aft
8																			
9	1			1		1		2			1			1		1		1	
10	2			2		2		2			2		1			2		1	
11	3			1		3		1			3			1		3		1	
12	4			2		4			2		4		2			4			1
13	5			2		5		1			5		1			5		1	
14	6			0		6		2			6		2			6		1	
15	7			0		7			1		7		1			7		1	
16	8			1		8		1			8		1			8		1	
17	9			1		9			1		9		1			9		1	
18	10		1			10		1			10		1			10		1	
19	11		1			11		1			11		1			11		1	
20	12		2			12		2			12		2			12		2	
21	13		1			13		1			13		1			13		1	
22	14		1			14		1			14		1			14		1	
23	15			1		15			1		15			1		15		1	
24	16		1			16		1			16		1			16		1	
25	17		2			17		2			17		2			17		2	
26	18		1			18		1			18		1			18		1	
27	19		1			19		1			19		1			19		1	
28	20		1			20		1			20		1			20		1	
29	Column Total		10	10				16	4				17	3				19	1
30	# Correct		8	5		# Correct		11	3		# Correct		13	3		# Correct		17	1
31	% Correct		40%	25%		% Correct		55%	15%		% Correct		65%	15%		% Correct		85%	5%
32	# Incorrect		2	3		# Incorrect		5	1		# Incorrect		4	0		# Incorrect		2	0
33	% Incorrect		10%	15%		% Incorrect		25%	5%		% Incorrect		20%	0%		% Incorrect		10%	0%
34	# No Response		0	2		# No Response		0	0		# No Response		0	0		# No Response		0	0
35	% No Response		0%	10%		% No Response		0%	0%		% No Response		0%	0%		% No Response		0%	0%
36																			
37	Total # Correct/B4			49		Total # No Resp/B4			0							Total # Incorrect/Aft		4	
38	Total % Correct/B4			61%		Total % No Resp/B4			0%							Total % Incorrect/Aft		5%	
39	Total # Incorrect/B4			13		Total # Correct/Aft			39							Total # No Resp/Aft		2	
40	Total % Incorrect/B4			65%		Total % Correct/Aft			49%							Total % No Resp/Aft		2%	
41	Date					Date					Date					Date			
42	Session 5					Session 6					Session 7					Session 8			
43	Start Time					Start Time					Start Time					Start Time			
44	Stop Time					Stop Time					Stop Time					Stop Time			
45	Total Time					Total Time					Total Time					Total Time			

Some data sheets require a specific structure. Therefore, it may be necessary to create more than one template for various types of data sheets. The example shown in Figure 5.9 is for a time-delay instructional procedure with a specific academic task: naming sight words. Therefore, this data sheet requires columns for the trial number, the stimulus word used, and the instructional action involved in that intervention (i.e., before prompt, after prompt, and a space between sessions). Spaces are also needed for the student's name;

FIGURE 5.10 Claris Works *Instructions for Data Sheet*

1. Open *Claris Works* and click your mouse on the spreadsheet.
2. Save the spreadsheet as "Data Sheet Template."
3. Format the spreadsheet under the Format menu to contain 19 columns and 39 rows.
4. Set the column widths as follows:
   Columns A, F, K, & P to 22;
   B, G, L, & Q to 48;
   C, D, E, H, I, J, M, N, O, R, & S to 20.
5. Set the default font to "Times" size 9.
6. Insert the heading centered over the spreadsheet with "Data Sheet: Time-Delay, Sight Words".
7. Enter "Date" in cell A1, "Session" in cell A2, "Start Time" in cell A3, "Stop Time" in cell A4, "Total Time" in cell A5, "Delay" in cell A6, "Trial" in cell A8, "Word" in cell B8, "B/4" in cell C8, "Aft" in cell D8, the number of the Trial (1 through 20) in cells A1 through A29, "# Correct" in cell A31, "% Correct" in cell A32, "# Incorrect" in cell A33, "% Incorrect" in cell A34, "# No Response" in cell A35, and "% No Response" in A36. This sets up the first set of columns for the data sheet.
8. Add sufficient spaces (out to 3½ inches on the ruler) to the right of the words "Date", "Session", "Start Time", "Stop Time", "Total Time", and "Delay". This provides a place to write this information.
9. Now you need to set up three other sets of columns for the data sheet.
   a. Select cells A1 to E35 and do a Copy.
   b. Select cell F1 and do a Paste.
   c. Select cell K1 and do a Paste.
   d. Select cell P1 and do a Paste.
10. To create the Key select "Install Footer" from the Format menu.
    a. Set a center tab and type "Key: + = Correct." Press Return.
    b. Type "− = Incorrect" under Correct.
    c. Type "0 = No Response" under Incorrect.

---

the teacher's name; the date; the session number; the start, stop, and total time; the number of correct, incorrect, and no responses; the percentage of correct, incorrect, and no responses; and a key.

You now have a template for a data sheet. Save this template as "Data Sheet Template." You can print this template to check the format or to use it in the classroom and save other copies. Remember to save your work after making any changes.

Graphing Behavior

Stand-alone programs are available to facilitate the analysis of behavior support data. One of the most efficient of these is *Cricket Graph III* (Computer Associates, 1992). The use of this program provides a more presentable graph than is available from "works" programs. It is also possible to edit the graphs created in *Cricket Graph III* to provide graphs that meet criteria for research publication. It will be necessary to export data from the "works" program to *Cricket Graph III* in order to analyze your data using this program. However, this is a relatively straightforward process explained in the manual.

Cricket Graph III is by no means the only graphing program available. However, when choosing a graphing program, the teacher should look for several attributes. For example, does the graphing program allow you to import data from the other CMI programs that you are already using? Are the instructions fairly easy to follow? Are the graphing capabilities sufficient for your needs? By asking yourself these questions, you should be able to purchase a graphing program that meets your needs.

Assessment and Instructional Planning with Expert Systems

In addition to the uses of computers already mentioned, there have been tremendous advances in technology-based assessment and instructional programming through application of expert systems to educational problems (Fuchs, Fuchs, & Hamlett, 1994; Greenwood, 1994; Irvin & Walker, 1994). These advances apply both to basic academic skills and to behavioral skills for all at-risk students and students with disabilities.

An *expert system* is a program that attempts to replicate the advice that an "expert" practitioner might give in a particular situation (Fuchs, Fuchs, & Hamlett, 1994). These computer-based systems typically contain tremendous amounts of information on a particular topic, and methods whereby that data can be interfaced with specific problem descriptions. These systems ask the educator certain questions and help him or her reach a conclusion or diagnosis. Expert systems are common in medicine. Also, there have been numerous advances in the expert systems associated with the assessment of students with special needs. Several of these were review by Greenwood and Rieth (1994). For example, there is now computer-based dynamic assessment of multidigit multiplication (Gerber, Semmel, & Semmel, 1994). Expert systems also exist to help teachers incorporate assessment results in their instructional planning (Fuchs, Fuchs, & Hamlett, 1994).

Perhaps a brief description of such an expert system would help illustrate these applications. An expert system called *SMH.PAL* can be used to help identify treatment procedures for students with severe disorders (Hofmeister, Althouse, Likins, Morgan, Ferrara, Jenson, & Rollins, 1994). To form this expert system, treatment interventions for a number of problem behaviors demonstrated by students with severe disabilities were selected from the research literature by a panel of experts. Initially, over 1,000 studies were reviewed, each of which demonstrated a research-proven treatment method for a single problem. Descriptions of these interventions were then included in the computerized database. Next, the creators developed a behavioral data-recording form that was designed to identify the specific behavioral problems demonstrated by a particular child, and to facilitate the discussion of those behaviors in terms of the treatment options included within the database. After a teacher completes the behavioral form, the use of the expert system will result in recommendations for specific treatments that are geared to the specific behaviors demonstrated by the child.

In conclusion, not only are computers helping with the day-to-day management of classrooms but they are also being used in assessing students' skills and in planning the educational interventions for these students. However, society is just starting to see the movement of computer technology into this area, and it remains to be seen what overall impact these expert systems will have on the education of at-risk students, or what the roll of the general education and special education teacher will be in the applications of these expert systems. Still, one may expect that the use of this technology will increase dramatically in the future.

Conclusion

In this chapter, we have tried to make classroom management easier through the use of computers. We gave instructions on creating an Attendance Roll and a Gradebook. Furthermore, Figures 5.2 and 5.4 detailed instructions for creating these using *Claris Works*. The instructions for these two tasks using any spreadsheet program will be similar. We also discussed how a word-processing program can make anecdotal report cards and letters to parents easier. Three programs that generate IEPs were discussed in some depth: *SEMS*, *Bonanza!*, and *Goal Rush*.

In the last section of this chapter, we talked about how computers could help with the collection, management, and analysis of student behavior. Steps to create a data collection sheet on a spreadsheet program were given. We also discussed about how computerized expert systems are being used in the assessment of students for determination of basic academic skills, as well as diagnosis and treatment planning for students with learning disabilities and behavioral disorders.

References

Fuchs, L. S., Fuchs, D., & Hamlett, C. L. (1994). Strengthening the Connection Between Assessment and Instructional Planning with Expert Systems. *Exceptional Children*, 61(2), 138–147.

Gerber, M. M., Semmel, D. S., & Semmel, M. I. (1994). Computer-Based Dynamic Assessment of Multidigit Multiplication. *Exceptional Children*, 61(2), 114–125.

Greenwood, C. R. (1994). Advances in Technology-Based Assessment within Special Education. *Exceptional Children*, 61(2), 102–104.

Greenwood, C. R., & Rieth, H. J. (1994). Current Dimensions of Technology-Based Assessment in Special Education. *Exceptional Children*, 61(2), 105–113.

Hofmeister, A. M., Althouse, R. B., Likins, M., Morgan, D. P., Ferrara, J. M., Jenson, W. R., & Rollins, E. (1994). SMH.PAL: An Expert System for Identifying Treatment Procedures for Students with Severe Disabilities. *Exceptional Children*, 61(2), 174–181.

Irvin, L. K., & Walker, H. M. (1994). Assessing Children's Social Skills Using Video-Based Microcomputer Technology. *Exceptional Children*, 61(2), 182–196.

6

Multimedia in the Classroom

Renet L. Bender
William N. Bender

*U*pon completion of this chapter you should be able to:

◆ Define multimedia.

◆ Identify the uses of multimedia.

◆ Identify the uses of authoring programs.

◆ Use HyperCard for creating software.

◆ Identify future uses of multimedia and CAI.

The technology of the future is here today in the form of multimedia. In fact, multimedia has already influenced education to the extent that the phrase *computer literacy* is being replaced by the phrase *technological literacy* in many school systems. *Multimedia* is the combination of several different types of media linked together by a computer and produced for viewing on the computer screen. The presentation media usually involved in multimedia are audio, text, videotape, print, and graphics. Furthermore, teachers can now utilize software that actually presents "moving pictures" on the individual computer.

Multimedia gives the user the power to jump from topic to topic and to change media at any time. Specifically, a student sitting at a computer would select a topic and be presented with a range of options. These may include reading technical material, viewing a four-minute filmstrip or videotape, developing a diagram for concept organization, and many other tasks. Each of these would be presented on the computer screen and would be under the moment-by-moment control of the student.

To better illustrate this important attribute of multimedia, consider the subject of history. Thirty years ago, a teacher could employ the use of filmstrips to teach certain topics in history. Filmstrips are said to be a *linear* medium, in that the film is viewed frame after frame. If a student is reminded of an associated topic by a particular frame, he or she must wait until the filmstrip is finished to pursue that associated topic through another medium. Most traditional classroom lessons are still linear in orientation. This means that material is presented, one topic after another, in the order that the teacher has chosen; students must follow along. In this sense, a traditional lesson may be viewed as a series of stepping stones across a pond. The students progress through the lesson like a person crossing the pond, one stepping stone at a time.

Multimedia lessons are not linear. When using multimedia, upon remembering an associated topic or the formulation of a question, the student can immediately redirect the content and access the informational resources on the computer regarding the associated topic or question. This means that at any time during the lesson, a student may view other information and return to the predefined lesson or continue on his or her self-selected branch of inquiry. So, rather than a series of predetermined stepping stones, one may view multimedia as a tree with many branches. All the students start with the same root and trunk but individual students may then branch out to other information at any time.

The method that many multimedia packages use for organization of information includes objects called *stacks* and *cards*. A stack can be thought of as a grouping of information such as a stack of index cards. A card in this analogy would represent a computer screen of information that may contain graphics, text, and buttons that allow the user to view other cards or show a video on the topic of choice. These buttons are usually specific areas on the screen that the student may either touch with a finger or click on with the mouse in order to make a selection. In a traditional or linear lesson, including traditional CAI lessons, the student would move through the stack of cards in order. However, in multimedia, the student may decide, because of his or her interest, to skip from card number 6 directly to card number 86, and then move back to card number 8. The student has the choice.

A stack may contain as many or as few cards as desired. Figure 6.1 is an example of a simple stack containing information on St. Augustine, Florida. The first card gives the student five options. By clicking the mouse on the button marked "Video," the student will see a video of a carriage tour along the harbor of St. Augustine. Clicking on "Settled," "Location," or "Climate" moves the student to the card (or screen) containing that information. By clicking on the arrow, he or she can move through the stack in a linear fashion.

In summary, multimedia is a compilation of related information utilizing several mediums. This information can be instantly accessed in any order or sequence. The process of accessing this information is called *hypermedia*. Thus, *multimedia* is sometimes referred to as *hypermedia*. Not all multimedia programs use all types of media and hypermedia, but they do all have one important characteristic: The user, not the program, directs the flow of the program.

This chapter on multimedia is important because the availability of these technologies can very much enhance learning for students with attention problems and low motivation. Many at-risk students can greatly benefit from multimedia since the pacing, attention, and motivational factors are under the individual student's control. Furthermore, the word *multimedia* can give some computer phobics a cold sweat. In most cases, a general knowledge can help ease the transition from older CAI programs to multimedia systems. We would like to encourage the teacher who feels overwhelmed by the idea of multimedia first to read briefly through this chapter and then start with a simple multimedia program that uses CD-ROM. Next, to come back to this chapter and read the parts of interest in more detail. It will not appear as daunting as before.

In this chapter, we explore the different types of media that usually comprise multimedia, including videodiscs, CD-ROMs, and class projection equipment. We then discuss the uses of multimedia. This is followed by a look at au-

FIGURE 6.1 **A Simple Stack**

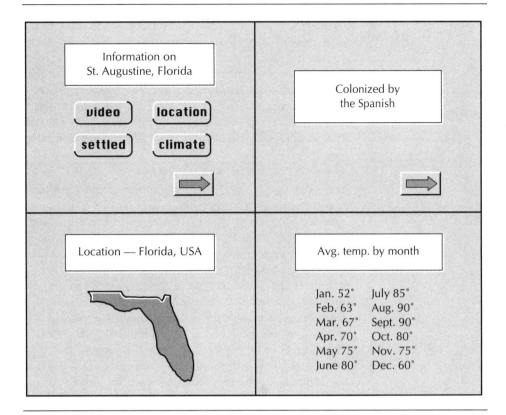

thoring systems, or the systems whereby a teacher may create a multimedia program, and one specific example of these programs, *HyperCard*. Finally, we will explore at the future use of computers with virtual reality.

Technology of Multimedia

Videodiscs

What Is a Videodisc?

Videodiscs (sometimes called *laserdiscs*) look like a 12-inch version of audio compact discs. Low-power light lasers are used to retrieve the information from them. Videodiscs differ significantly from the usual floppy disk (Lewis, 1993) in several ways. First, videodiscs store text, graphics, and video rather than merely numeric data like a floppy disk. Second, videodiscs can store considerably more information than a floppy disk or a hard drive. Third, videodiscs are an optical medium, in that the information contained on the disk is read by a low-power light laser. Finally, unlike floppy disks, one can only read information from a video disc—that is, one typically cannot write to a videodisc.

Videodisc Formats

Videodiscs are made with two formats. A *format* is a map put on the videodisc that tells the videodisc player how the information is stored on the disc. The two formats for videodiscs are continuous linear velocity and continuous angular velocity, referred to as CLV and CAV, respectively.

Videodiscs with CLV format can hold the most information of the two formats. CLV videodiscs can contain up to 60 minutes of video per side, but the information is indexed by time (time is the length of time from the beginning of the disc to the information desired). Time segments on the disc are accessed by barcode readers similar to the ones found in the check-out lines at grocery stores. This method of accessing information is slow and is usually not used when a high rate of interactivity is required.

Videodiscs with CAV format may contain as much as 54,000 frames, or 30 minutes of video per side. Information is quickly accessed by the individual frame or group of frames desired. CAV format is preferred for interactive use in classrooms since this format allows for quicker access of individual frames and freezing of pictures without loss of picture quality.

Videodisc Presentation Systems

Both of these formats can be used in systems consisting of the videodisc player and a monitor or television, called *stand-alone systems*. Using this type of method, one can only play the videodisc in the same manner VCR tapes are played, from start to finish. CLV and CAV formats can also be used in interactive systems. Interactive use requires a videodisc player, a monitor with speaker, and a computer. Interactive systems allow for quick access to all information on the videodisc in a nonlinear fashion.

When used interactively, the videodisc is controlled by a software program called a *navigator* or an *authoring program*. This program helps to organize the information on the videodisc in a way that allows easy access by the users (Lewis, 1993). It allows the user to put together text and graphics, as well as to skip through the content to find the needed information. When used interactively, the videodisc can be used as an initial instruction aide for students, and this makes the technology a much more powerful teaching tool for at-risk students.

CD-ROM Disks

CD-ROM disks represent the newest technology for storing large amounts of data and text. (These disks were briefly discussed in Chapter 3.) CD-ROM disks look like CDs that play music, except CD-ROM disks are used to store not only sound but also pictures, video, and text. CD-ROM drives can be purchased as an add-on for your computer system or they may be included in the system. This type of disk is popular for storing reference material such as specialized encyclopedias, art libraries, and simulation programs. The material may then be referenced by a student working alone or by a teacher for use in preparing a lesson. CD-ROM drives can be an integral part of authoring systems and interactive multimedia systems (discussed later in this chapter).

Audio Digitizers

Audio is an important part of the multimedia experience. It can include music, sound effects, and voice. Many multimedia applications include high-quality prerecorded sound. However, in some cases, users may have the option of recording their own sound—a process that is accomplished using a device called an audio digitizer. Audio digitizers convert sound to digital signals. The user has the option of using audio from tapes played into the microphone of the audio digitizer.

Digital Scanners

Unmoving visual images can be incorporated in multimedia in a variety of ways. Some multimedia software has graphics packages that allow the user to draw pictures, and some allow the use of pictures from laserdiscs or CD-ROMs. The user can also create his or her own computer images with a device called a digital scanner. Scanners make computer-ready copies of flat visual images such as photographs and illustrations from books. A user can scan maps, cartoons, and printed material.

There are two basic types of scanners: the flat-bed type that looks like a copier and the hand-held type. Most classrooms that have scanners use the hand-held type because they are less expensive.

Projection Systems

The output of multimedia programs includes the visual information seen on the computer monitor and the sound from the computer's speaker. The usual computer monitor and speaker works fine when one person or a small group of people are using the system but some modifications may be needed if the system is to be used with the entire class. Sound can be amplified by adding

FIGURE 6.2 *Using an LCD Panel in the Classroom*

Reprinted by permission of In Focus Systems.

FIGURE 6.3 *List of Multimedia Products and Resources*

In Focus Systems, Inc.
7770 SW Mohawk Street
Tualatin, OR 97062
1–800–294–6400

*The Educator's Guide to HyperCard
and HyperTalk*
by George H. Culp and G. Morgan Watkins
(Allyn and Bacon)

Quest Multimedia Authoring System
Allen Communication, Inc.
Lakeside Plaza II
5225 Wiley Post Way
Salt Lake City, UT 84116
1–801–537–7800

Activision
P.O. Box 3048
Menlo Park, CA 94025–3047
414–329–7699

Intellimation Library for the Macintosh
130 Cremon Drive
P.O. Box 1922
Santa Barbara, CA 93116
800–3-INTELL

Sharp Electronics Corporation
Sharp Plaza
P.O. Box 650
Mahwah, NJ 07430–2135
1–201–529–8200

Hypermedia!NOW
Randall Boone or Kyle Higgins
College of Education
University of Nevada
4505 Maryland Parkway
Las Vegas, NV 89154
1–702–895–4687

Hyperstudio
Roger Wagner Publishing Inc.
1050 Pioneer Way, Suite P
El Cajon, CA 92020
1–619–442–0522

Claris Corporation
5201 Patrick Henry Drive
Box 58168
Santa Clara, CA 95052–8168
415–960–1500

Print and Graphics Educational Systems
450 Taraval Street, #235
San Francisco, CA 94116
415–665–3924

external speakers to the computer system. Some systems are even capable of stereo sound.

When teachers want to use multimedia in a lesson for the entire class, they have several options. One option is to have a computer that has a large monitor or can be plugged into a large television screen that everyone can see. The second alternative is to utilize an LCD panel such as the one from In Focus Systems. This type of device is seen in Figure 6.2. The In Focus Systems LCD panel is plugged into the computer and placed on top of an overhead projector. The result is that whatever is on the monitor is shown on the projection screen at the front of the class. The education series of In Focus LCD panels consists of three LCD panels: a black and white version, a color version with 16 colors, and a second color version with photographic colors. These panels range in price from $1,500 to $3,500. Information on In Focus can be found in Figure 6.3 (a list of multimedia products and resources). Sharp also offers a wide variety of LCD panels that range in price from $1,200 to $5,000.

Can Students Learn from Multimedia?

Hofmeister (1989) points out that most teachers spend half of their time in front of the class and the other half in instructional interactions with their students. With the use of videodisc players and well-designed videodiscs, teachers can spend much more of their time interacting with individual students, while directing the presentation using a remote control from any point in the classroom.

One use of videodiscs involves implementation of inclusive classrooms for students who are at-risk for educational problems. *Mastering Fractions,* one of the Core Concepts videodisc programs, is an example of such a program (Miller & Cooke, 1989; Lubke, Rogers, & Evans, 1989). This program uses direct instruction (as described by Gersten, Carnine, & Woodard, 1987) to teach fractions to at-risk students. The direct instructional principles emphasized include the explicit teaching of "general case" problem-solving strategies, development of mastery at each step in the process, strategy corrections for student errors, gradual fading from teacher-directed activities toward independent work, use of systematic practice with a range of examples, and cumulative review of newly learned concepts.

Due to the careful planning of this videodisc program, it has been shown (in study after study) to be effective in teaching large and diverse classes, including at-risk students (Miller & Cooke, 1989; Hofmeister, Engelmann, & Carnine, 1986; Kelly, Carnine, & Grossen, 1986; Hasselbring et al., 1987; Meskill, 1987; Petersen, Hofmeister, & Lubke, 1988). These studies conclude that almost all of the at-risk students performed within the range of scores of the regular education students using this technology. Thus, the use of these technologies could certainly enhance efforts toward inclusion of at-risk students in mainstream classes. In most of these studies, the at-risk students were in a large group, without any special help or private remediation. These studies demonstrate that high-quality videodisc instruction may be appropriate for both special and regular education students.

This research also demonstrated several special benefits for at-risk students who were mainstreamed. Kelly, Carnine, and Grossen (1986) suggested that videodisc instruction may help to prepare students for mainstreaming or inclusive classrooms. Also, Miller and Cooke (1989) reported positive comments about the program from numerous students. Most of the students involved made comments such as, "I liked it a lot" and "It was easier." At-risk students' comments included statements such as "It (videodisc instruction) didn't treat me different," "I felt like I could keep up," and "I liked it (having a combined class)."

In summary, using high-quality multimedia instruction can facilitate inclusion of at-risk students and allows the teacher to assume the role of instruction manager. As instruction manager, the teacher is free to circulate, monitor students' work, and provide immediate feedback for correct and incorrect responses during the presentation. Other advantages reported in the use of videodiscs (Lubke, Rogers, & Evans, 1989) include the following: Students seem more motivated, lessons can be replayed for individual students, and the circulating teacher is able to correct the student errors immediately, thus providing timely feedback.

Uses of Multimedia

This section will examine the uses of commercially available multimedia packages. A multimedia system for your classroom need not be expensive (Yarrow, 1994). You can start with a minimal system that supports a program such as *HyperCard* (discussed later in the chapter) and a clip-art program. In this section, we will give you some ideas on how to use multimedia that have been developed by others, and an idea of the variety of products on the market.

Wilson (1991) suggested three potential classroom uses for preexisting multimedia packages.

1. *Teacher presentations, using a large-screen monitor or projection device.* In this application, the teacher uses the multimedia system to help him or her present the lesson. For example, while presenting a lesson in astronomy, the teacher could use *RedShift Multimedia Astronomy* by Maris Multimedia Ltd. to show movement of the planets, moons, and other objects. This multimedia package includes videos taken by the Moon Rover vehicle and serves as a high-interest instructional tool for at-risk students.

2. *Student exploration, inquiry, hypothesis testing, and research.* With this interactive use of multimedia, students can use information on CD-ROMs such as a specialized encyclopedia to learn about a topic. This allows students to proceed at their own pace, which greatly enhances the applicability of this tool for at-risk students.

3. *Student authoring or producing multimedia reports.* In this application, the students are required to use an authoring system, such as *Hyper-Card,* to put together a report on a specific topic. This creative activity could also be assigned as a cooperative group project.

Teacher Presentations

When teachers want to use multimedia in an academic lesson, they have several options. One option is to place a computer at a central location in the classroom and have students huddle around it. Another option is to have groups of students use various computers in the classroom. A number of teachers are moving toward several more recently developed options. A teacher may arrange a computer in the classroom with a large monitor that everyone can see. Finally, teachers may utilize an LCD panel.

The preparation time involved in using multimedia is minimal. Before the lesson, the teacher should locate the videodisc or information that he or she wishes to show the class during the lesson. The information may also be on a CD-ROM disc. In most cases, the discs have a manual that includes a list of the information and barcodes that, when scanned, will show specific information on the monitor. During the lesson, the teacher would need only to scan the proper barcode to display the information for the class.

Student Exploration, Inquiry, and Hypothesis Testing

Traditionally, when students wanted to learn about a topic or find an answer to a question, they went to the library. In the library they had access to books, journals, and films. Today, students have access to information on many topics in their classrooms in the form of CD-ROMs and videodiscs. In addition to presenting information at their fingertips, the information is not linear, as it is in traditional media. For example, while a student is reading the answer to one question, he or she may think of a second question. Rather than stopping and finding a book with information on the second question, the student can immediately research the second question without getting up. When the student is finished with the second question, he or she can return to the first topic or continue with other topics. For students with attention difficulties and organizational problems, these immediate access features may be either a blessing or a curse. It will help many at-risk students to immediately access topics of interest, but teachers should monitor the student's selections to assure that students remain on the several "stacks" of information that the teacher wants them to access. In other words, students with organizational problems can "get lost" among the numerous options presented by multimedia.

Examples of information available on CD-ROMs and videodiscs include *Anatomy & Physiology* by Videodiscovery on a videodisc. This package, which is three dimensional, uses animation to let students observe human structure in detail; it even includes simulations of dissections.

Another example is *Geopedia* by Encyclopedia Britannica Educational Corporation on CD-ROM discs. This encyclopedia package features pictures, maps, charts, graphs, and tables.

Student Authoring

Multimedia presentations can be done with *HyperCard*. Yarrow (1994) recommends reinforcing subject matter by having students create interactive tutorials using **HyperCard.** Students usually spend six weeks learning this system. Initially, students are paired together and each pair selects a topic from one of the classes with which to create an interactive tutorial. The students are encouraged to use text, pictures, graphics, sound, and animation in their presentations. The first part of the assignment is for each group to create an outline of their stack. The students are limited to three subroutines of information, with each routine having six questions in a multiple-choice or true/false format. Most student groups follow the format of presenting information in a creative way and then asking a question. This format provides the user with an interactive strategy that includes immediate reinforcement.

In addition to this assignment, Yarrow also suggests using *HyperCard* with language arts. This may include using *HyperCard* to create tutorials for grammar or developing interactive stories that will heighten the reading experience for at-risk learners.

Authoring Programs

A fourth use of multimedia in the classroom is teacher creation of multimedia lessons (Wilson, 1991; Monti, Cicchetti, Goodkind, & Ganci, 1994). Teacher-made materials can range from something as simple as digitizing an image for a lesson to creating a lesson or electronic text for reading. When creating a lesson or electronic text, teachers can start from scratch, using an authoring system such as *HyperCard*, or they may modify existing materials.

Authoring systems allow teachers to combine information from different sources such as pictures, charts, films, books and audio into one multimedia package controlled by a computer. Using authoring systems, teachers can create computer-based lessons utilizing their own content and presentation features for individual students. Authoring systems range from programs that provide a lesson template, or form, to those that allow the user to create his or her lesson from scratch (an example of this type is *HyperCard*).

Authoring programs that are used to create multimedia lessons are sometimes called *hypermedia-authoring* programs. Examples of these programs include *HyperCard* by Claris (Macintosh computers), *Linkway* by IBM (IBM and IBM compatible computers), and *HyperStudio* by Roger Wagner (Apple IIe/GS computers). They allow for the integration of text, graphics, sound, and video into one package by the development of hypertext. The hypertext is developed by creating cards or stacks of information that are linked together by the computer. The user (or author) determines which information should be linked and interrelated. Most of these programs have stacks already available to help teachers with the design of individualized lessons.

Hypermedia-authoring systems are great for flexibility and creativity. But these systems are time consuming to learn and use. To create lessons requires a knowledge of CAI design skills and screen design. If you use ready-made stacks, then the amount of time you spend designing the lessons can be considerably reduced.

Hypermedia!Now

Boone, Higgins, Falba, and Langley developed the software *Hypermedia!NOW*, which requires *HyperCard* to run. This software was developed with a federal grant and is free to teachers. They included a copy of *Hypermedia!NOW* on disk with their paper in *LD Forum* (fall 1993 issue). This software is specifically designed to help teachers and students create their own hypermedia cooperative texts.

Boone, Higgins, Falba, and Langley (1993) recommended using a multimedia environment in a cooperative framework for reading and writing. In this electronic text program, students can touch a word that is unfamiliar and immediately see the definition and hear the pronunciation. Through electronic texts, students have immediate access to supplemental data without having to seek additional help outside of the immediate reading environment. Furthermore, the supplemental information can be in the form of text, sound, speech, graphics, video, or a combination of these. The "electronic book" is comprised of 10 pages each with a picture of a notepad on which text can be entered and read. Emphasized or boldface words allow the student to activate up to four branches per page. An example of this is seen in Figure 6.4.

FIGURE 6.4 Sample of an Electronic Text

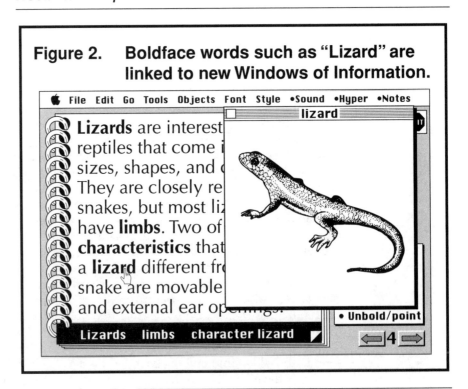

Source: Reprinted with permission from Boone, R., Higgins, K., Falba, C., & Langley, W. (1993). *LD Forum, 19*(1), Council for Learning Disabilities.

Technically, *Hypermedia!NOW* is a specially designed stack for use with *HyperCard*. In Figure 6.5, you can see that each page of the "book" has several parts. These parts include the typical menu bar with a few additional options such as Sound, Hyper, and Notes. The first two of these options are used as the book is being written. The Notes option is a notebook in which the user can write notes as he or she reads the book.

FIGURE 6.5   *Components of an Electronic Text*

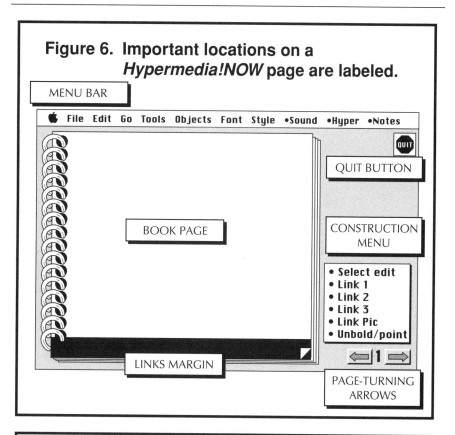

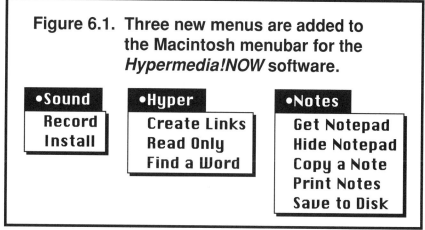

Source: Reprinted with permission from Boone, R., Higgins, K., Falba, C., & Langley, W. (1993). *LD Forum, 19*(1), Council for Learning Disabilities.

Boone, Higgins, Falba, and Langley included step-by-step instructions on constructing a hypermedia page and setting *HyperCard* memory. These are presented in Figures 6.6 and 6.7. *Hypermedia!NOW* can be run on Macintosh computers.

FIGURE 6.6   *Instructions for Constructing a Hypermedia Page*

To Begin:

Create a duplicate of the **HyperMedia!NOW** original template stack using the **duplicate** item from the **file** menu. Rename the new stack "Myths."

Double click on the "Myths" icon to open the stack. After the credits are given, **click on** the right arrow to move to page 1 of the hypermedia electronic book.

Choose **create links** from the **Hyper** menu.

Entering Text:

Click on **Select/edit** in the construction menu located at the right of the screen. Then **click into** the top area of the blank book page.

Type the following page of text:

Myths have been the basis of great literature and art through the ages. The Greek gods looked like mortals, but were taller, more beautiful, and could do no wrong. They lived on top of Mt. Olympus. Zeus was the most powerful of the Greek gods.

Linking Words:

Click on **Select/edit** and move to the page of text to **highlight** the word "Myths." **Holding** the mouse button down and **dragging** the 1-beam cursor across the word will highlight it.

Click on **Link 1** in the construction menu. A sound reminder will be heard each time a link has been created.

Click on **select/edit** again. **Highlight** the word "mortals" and **click on Link 2** in the construction menu.

Click on **select/edit**. **Highlight** the two words "Mt. Olympus." Before the words can be linked, they must be grouped. While the words are highlighted, **go to** menu item **style** in the top menubar and **choose Group**. Then **click on link 3** in the construction menu.

Click on **select/edit** again. **Highlight** the word "Zeus" and **click on link pic**.

The boldface words are now "buttons" that are linked to the pop-up text and graphic windows.

Typing Definitions and Explanations:

Once the button links have been created, definitions or other information can be typed into the pop-up text windows.

Click on the bold word "myths" on the hypermedia book page. Be sure to have the "hand" cursor (click on **unbold/point** if you need to get it). A window labeled "linked field #1" will appear.

Highlight the words "linked field #1" and press the delete key. Then type this definition:

Myths are imaginary stories that explain practices, beliefs, or natural phenomena from the point of view of a culture of people.

Click on the hypermedia book page to make the window disappear. Don't click on another boldfaced word when clicking to close a window. This will cause a second pop-up window to appear. If this happens, just click twice on the book page to clear both windows.

For the second button, **click on** the bold word "mortals" in the text to make the window labeled "linked field #2" appear. **Delete** the label by highlighting it and using the delete key. Enter the definition:

Mortals are human beings with the characteristics of men and women.

FIGURE 6.6 **Continued**

Click on the hypermedia book page to make the window disappear. **Click on** the bold words "Mt. Olympus" to make "linked field #3" appear. **Delete** the window label by highlighting and using the delete key. Type the following information:

Mt. Olympus is a mountain so high and steep that no mortal could climb it. In the palace on Mt. Olympus there was always light.

Now for the last link, the button will show the picture file named "zeus." When the user clicks on the bold word "Zeus," the graphic will appear because the **HyperMedia!NOW** disk already contains a picture file named "Zeus." Without a picture file, the program displays a message asking where the file can be found. The name of the picture file must match the button word exactly to show the graphic.

Click on the "close square" in the upper left corner of the graphic window to close it. Clicking on the page will not close graphic windows. The first page of this stack is now ready. This electronic book can be continued by moving on to page 2 and entering new text and links.

Source: Reprinted with permission from Boone, R., Higgins, K., Falba, C., & Langley, W. (1993). *LD Forum, 19*(1), Council for Learning Disabilities.

Figure 6.7 **Setting HyperCard Memory**

The HyperCard application's memory allocation limit is quite low as it comes installed initially on a Macintosh. This memory limit is totally independent of the amount of RAM memory installed in the computer. To use the recording function in **Hypermedia!NOW** it is necessary to increase the memory allocation of the **HyperCard** application to a minimum of 1,000 K. The following is a step-by-step description of this process.

1. Click once on the **HyperCard** application icon. It will darken.
2. Choose "Get info" from the "File" menu. An information window will appear.
3. Click the mouse into the "Current size" box at the bottom of the window. Replace the number in the box with "1000".
4. Click on the "close box" in the upper left corner of the window.

The new larger memory allocation will take effect the next time **HyperCard** is opened.

Source: Reprinted with permission from Boone, R., Higgins, K., Falba, C., & Langley, W. (1993). *LD Forum, 19*(1), Council for Learning Disabilities.

Development of Multimedia

In the development of CAI lessons using hypermedia-authoring systems, 60 to 80 percent of the time is spent on planning (Sampath & Quaine, 1990; Steinberg, 1984). Fitzgerald, Bauder, and Werner (1992) list the prerequisite skills and a seven-step systematic planning model for developing hypermedia stacks. To be able to produce high-quality CAI lessons, knowledge of three areas is required (Sampath & Quaine, 1990):

1. Subject matter
2. An authoring program
3. Systematic instructional design

Figure 6.8 (Fitzgerald, Bauder, & Werner, 1992) shows the Courseware Authoring Process Model (Fitzgerald, 1989), which is similar to other instructional design and development models based on the systems approach suggested by Gagne and Briggs (1979). The particular model shown is

FIGURE 6.8 Courseware Authoring Process

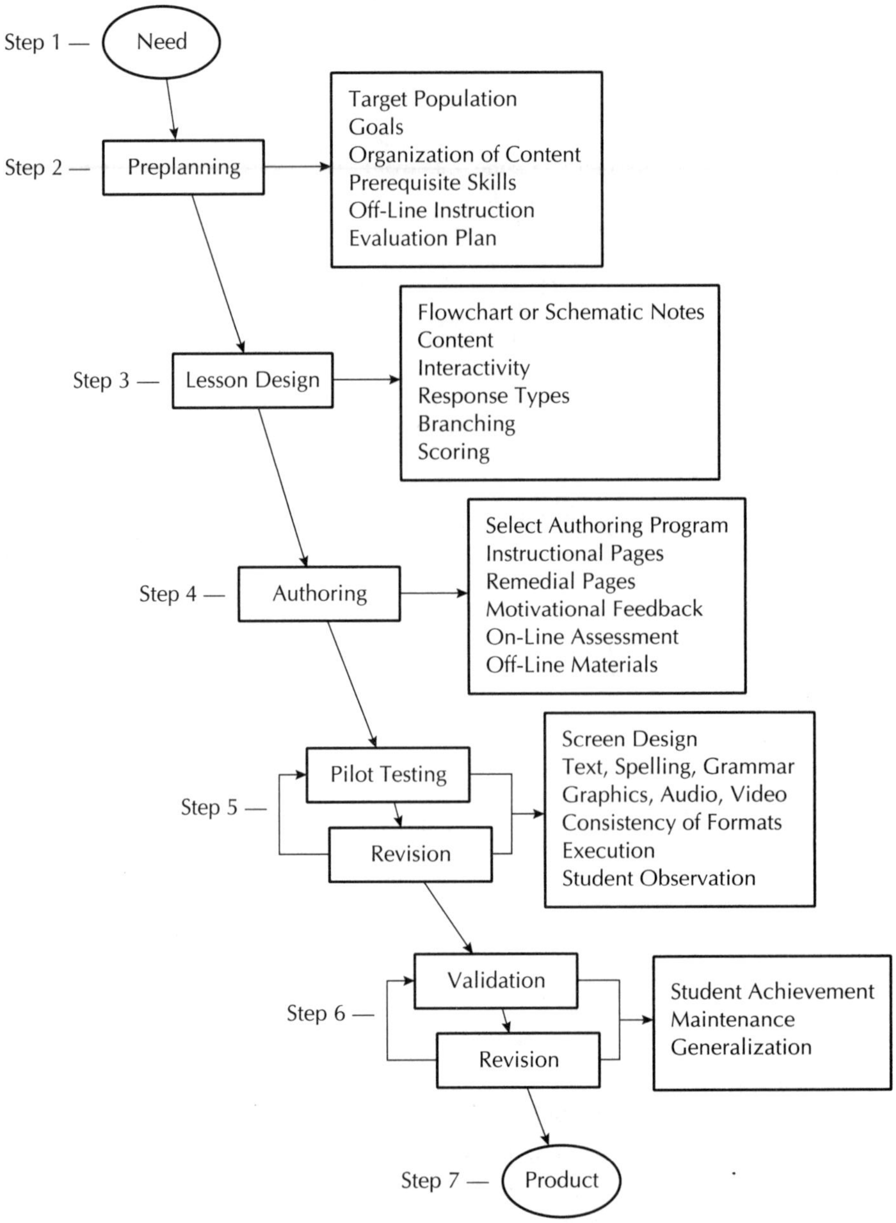

Step 1 — (Need)

Step 2 — Preplanning → Target Population / Goals / Organization of Content / Prerequisite Skills / Off-Line Instruction / Evaluation Plan

Step 3 — Lesson Design → Flowchart or Schematic Notes / Content / Interactivity / Response Types / Branching / Scoring

Step 4 — Authoring → Select Authoring Program / Instructional Pages / Remedial Pages / Motivational Feedback / On-Line Assessment / Off-Line Materials

Step 5 — Pilot Testing / Revision → Screen Design / Text, Spelling, Grammar / Graphics, Audio, Video / Consistency of Formats / Execution / Student Observation

Step 6 — Validation / Revision → Student Achievement / Maintenance / Generalization

Step 7 — (Product)

Source: From "Authoring CAI Lessons: Teachers as Developers" by G. E. Fitzgerald, D. K. Bauder, and J. G. Werner, *Teaching Exceptional Children, 24* (2) (1992) (pages 15–21). Copyright 1992 by The Council for Exceptional Children. Reprinted with permission.

designed to be used with the hypermedia-authoring systems currently in use in schools.

Step 1. *Determine the need for authoring courseware.* Before jumping into creating software, Fitzgerald, Bauder and Werner (1992) suggest that teachers should justify the time that will be spent in the development of the courseware. They recommend consideration of authoring courseware if appropriate instructional materials cannot be found among available software or if special instructional or hardware capabilities are needed. The development time should be evaluated in terms of anticipated student gains and projected use of materials.

Step 2. *Preplan the content and curriculum correspondence.* The preplanning stage should be used to organize the scope and sequence of the lesson. When working on the preplanning stage, Fitzgerald, Bauder, and Werner give several details that must be considered.

1. *Determine the target population.* This helps to establish the conceptual level, readability, age appropriateness, and functional application.
2. *Set goals for the program.* Write goals in terms of measurable instructional objectives.
3. *Content should be identified and organized.* In organizing the content, it can be done in the form of an outline. Content should be placed in the sequence desired for the lesson.
4. *Prerequisite skills needed by the student should be identified.*
5. *A method of evaluation must be developed for students.* This should include a pre-and posttest or criterion-based measures.
6. *The integration of the lesson should be planned.* This may include worksheets, teaching plans, introductory material, and resources required.

As we have iterated throughout this book, the learning characteristics of at-risk students are more involved and complex than for the nondisabled or average population. Careful consideration should be given to the characteristics discussed throughout the book, including attention problems, motivation, self-concept, and so on.

Step 3. *Design the CAI lesson.* The design phase includes the presentation of the lesson, the type and amount of interaction with the student, and branching. Teachers must also decide what data to collect and how to collect it. In this phase of development, teachers must produce a detailed and comprehensive design of the lesson. Fitzgerald, Bauder, and Werner (1992) suggest the use of a graphic plan to keep track of the links between the screens. An example of such a graphic for a multiple-choice question is seen in Figure 6.9 (Fitzgerald, Bauder, & Werner, 1992).

Step 4. *Create the lesson.* This is where teachers use their knowledge of a hypermedia-authoring system to create the lesson. Note that since hypermedia-authoring systems differ, teachers may have to modify the design of the lesson depending on the authoring system chosen. Also included in this step is the development of assessment activities and noncomputer materials, such as worksheets, to be used with the lesson. These types of materials are referred to as *off-line materials* since they are not available on the computer.

Step 5. *Test the lesson and make revisions.* The purpose of this step is to find out if the lesson works as planned. Fitzgerald, Bauder, and Werner (1992) suggest that this step be carried out in two parts. The first part is to have the lesson reviewed by a colleague who tries out all the answers, error paths, and links. Form 6.1 may be used as a guide (Fitzgerald, 1989). The second part is to test the lesson with students after it is working smoothly. The goal for this part of the testing is to check for confusion or operational difficulties.

FIGURE 6.9 *Flowchart for Multiple-Choice Question*

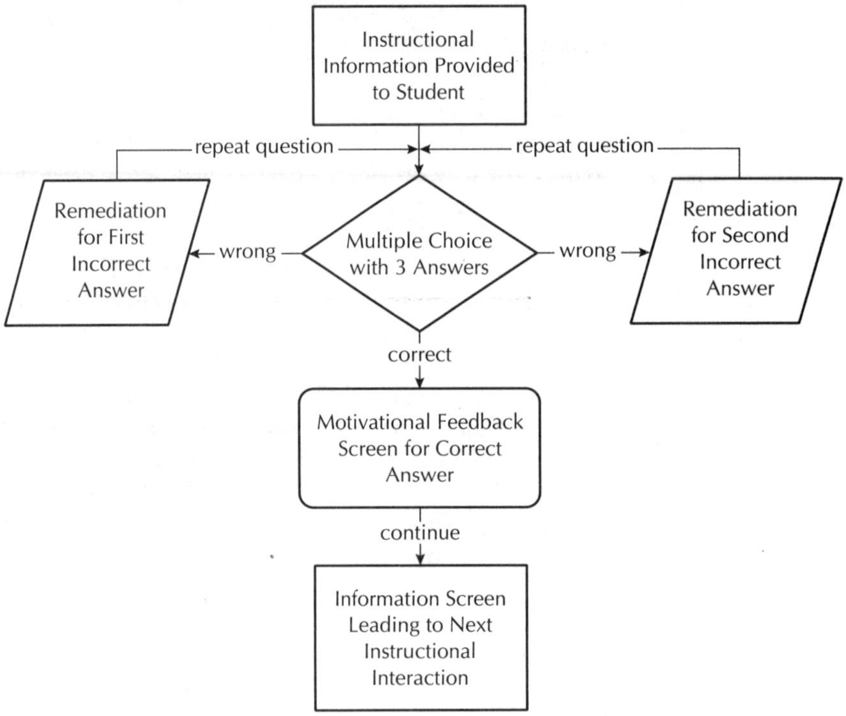

Source: From "Authoring CAI Lessons: Teachers as Developers" by G. E. Fitzgerald, D. K. Bauder, and J. G. Werner, *Teaching Exceptional Children, 24* (2) (1992) (pages 15–21). Copyright © 1992 by The Council for Exceptional Children. Reprinted with permission.

Step 6. *Validate lesson outcomes and revisions.* Students who are at-risk should use the lesson from start to finish, including off-line materials and testing. Review of the outcome of these results will suggest further revisions. This validation phase will also indicate if there is a need for further lesson development.

Step 7. *Package development.* In this step, you need to document the lesson that you have developed. This should include a written description of its objectives and content, the students for whom the lesson was developed, prerequisite skills, implementation guidelines, and supportive instructional materials.

FORM 6.1

Guide Sheet for Review of CAI Lessons Developed with Authoring Systems

Grade the multimedia software on each of the items listed below on a scale of 0–5 with 0 being the worst and 5 excellent.

Initial Plan

_____ 1. Target population.

_____ 2. Goals and objective.

_____ 3. Organization and sequencing of content.

_____ 4. Task analysis within components.

_____ 5. Identification of prerequisite skills.

_____ 6. Flowchart: Completeness, accuracy.

_____ 7. Initial evaluation plan.

_____ 8. Planned integration with off-line instruction.

Lesson Design

_____ 1. Opening conveys objectives to student.

_____ 2. Flow of lesson: Logical and provides necessary transition.

_____ 3. Interactivity: High level of student responding and choices.

_____ 4. Use of remediation for errors and signals to teacher for help.

_____ 5. Accuracy of destinations to implement flowchart as designed.

_____ 6. Consistency of response types to questions.

_____ 7. Closing: Provides summary and generalization.

_____ 8. Recordkeeping/scoring accuracy for intent.

Screen Design

_____ 1. Adequate white space around graphics and blocks of text.

_____ 2. Clear visual separation of text and response prompts.

_____ 3. Readability of text: Size, screen placement, no split words.

_____ 4. Use of colors and highlighting for cueing.

_____ 5. Use of graphics to aid conceptualization and for cueing.

_____ 6. Proper grammar and correct spelling.

_____ 7. Consistency of symbols, formats, and fonts throughout lesson.

Source: From "Authoring CAI Lessons: Teachers as Developers" by G. E. Fitzgerald, D. K. Bauder, and J. G. Werner, *Teaching Exceptional Children, 24* (2) (1992) (pages 15–21). Copyright 1992 by The Council for Exceptional Children. Reprinted with permission.

Evaluation of Multimedia Software

Instruction using multimedia is promising but unless the motivational properties of the program are effective, the full benefits will not be obtained. Keller and Keller (1994) combined four components of interactivity with the primary features of a motivational design model into a checklist that can be used to design and evaluate multimedia programs. The authors have defined interactivity as the kind, amount, and timing of interaction in an instructional program. Furthermore, they divided interactivity into four areas (Keller & Keller, 1994):

1. *Learner control.* Learner control involves the pacing, sequencing, and selection of the instructional material by the student. For example, this includes what selections a student may make and when material is reviewed.
2. *Stimulus characteristics.* Stimulus characteristics include the material presented and how it is presented.
3. *Learner responses.* Learner responses include the emotional responses as well as the mechanical responses such as solving problems and note taking.
4. *Consequences.* Consequences include the actions the program takes as a result of student responses.

The motivational design model that Keller and Keller use is the ARCS model (Keller, 1987a, 1987b). This model has four criteria that must be met for a lesson to stimulate and sustain the motivation to learn in a student. First, the student's attention must be obtained. Second, the lesson must build relevance by connecting the lesson to the student's experiences. Third, the lesson should allow the student to build confidence that he or she will succeed in the lesson. Fourth, the student must receive some degree of satisfaction from his or her learning experience.

The checklist in Form 6.2 was developed by Keller and Keller (1994) and combines the preceding components of interactivity and the ARCS model of motivational design. The checklist consists of two parts. The Management Interactivity part applies to learner control. The second part, Instructional Interactivity, applies to the motivational responses in the student and the feedback that the student receives.

FORM 6.2

Motivating Interactivity in Multimedia (The MIM Checklist)
Bonnie H. Keller & John M. Keller

Introduction

This checklist contains motivational tactics that have been demonstrated to have a positive motivational effect when used appropriately in interactive multimedia instruction. The purpose of the checklist is to assist in planning and evaluating multimedia instruction with respect to interactivity. There are two major parts to the checklist. The first pertains to those tactics that apply primarily to learner control over managing the multimedia instructional program, and the second pertains more to features that affect the degree of motivation in the instructional interactivity.

Each item in this checklist has been categorized as to whether its primary effect is on stimulating or maintaining attention (A), establishing relevance (R), developing confidence (C), or building satisfaction (S) in the learner. Some items may appeal to more than one of these categories. For additional information on this approach to identifying and categorizing motivational tactics, see the reference at the end of this checklist.

Instructions

Three columns are provided for your use. You may modify them to suit your requirements.

Applies? Put a check in this column if a given tactic applies to the given program of multimedia instruction. There are numerous criteria that may be used to make this decision.

Present? This coumn can be used when reviewing progress during development or when evaluating finished products. It simply indicates whether a given tactic has been incorporated as planned. If the tactic is included in the materials, but was not checked as applying to the audience, then consider removing it.

Rating? Use any rating scale that you wish. For example, a simple S for satisfactory or U for unsatisfactory works in some situations. In others, reviewers prefer to use a five point scale ranging from excellent (exceeds requirements) to unacceptable.

Management Interactivity

Applies?	Present?	Rating?		
			1.	**Pacing: Program characteristics that allow learner control over pacing.**
_____	_____	_____	1.1	Learners have control over when and how fast to move through the program or have the option to exercise such control if desired. (A, S)
			2.	**Override: Program characteristics that allow learners to override, or interrupt, the program sequence.**
_____	_____	_____	2.1	Learners have access to system help at all times. (C)
_____	_____	_____	2.2	Learners may exit instructional presentations or practice exercises when they wish. (S)
			3.	**Selection: Program characteristics that allow learner control over sequencing and structure.**

Applies?	*Present?*	*Rating?*		
_____	_____	_____	3.1	System navigational skills are prerequisite or an easy tutorial is provided. (C)
_____	_____	_____	3.2	Instructional framework and levels are as easy as possible to move through (include only the levels required for course complexity). (C)
_____	_____	_____	3.3	Learners may review presentations and practice as often as they wish. (C)
_____	_____	_____	3.4	Diagnostic checkpoints are provided before major portions of instruction and practice, and learners who perform satisfactorily may move ahead. (A, S)
_____	_____	_____	3.5	Learners have access to the main menu as often as possible. (A, S)
_____	_____	_____	3.6	A predetermined selection and sequence is recommended but not required. (A, R, S)

4. Internal Motivation: Program characteristics to stimulate motivated internal learner responses:

_____	_____	_____	4.1	Mystery, paradox, or inquiry is used to introduce segments which may be inherently less interesting to learners. (A)
_____	_____	_____	4.2	Instructional segments are varied in length and speed. (A)
_____	_____	_____	4.3	Appealing and clear graphics are provided to break up text blocks and/or to communicate information. (A)
_____	_____	_____	4.4	Adequate time is allowed for covert responding. (A, C)
_____	_____	_____	4.5	Role-plays, games, and simulations have characters and settings appropriate for characteristics of learners, and their interest and contain content and applications related to the objectives. (A, R)
_____	_____	_____	4.6	Scenarios and case studies contain human interest (good characterizations), realistic situations, problems appropriate for the objectives and content, and are appropriate for current skill level of learners. (A, R, C)
_____	_____	_____	4.7	Examples are provided for all relevant learner contexts. (R)
_____	_____	_____	4.8	The relationship between program content and dealing with common fears and misconceptions is made explicit. (C)
_____	_____	_____	4.9	Introductions or overviews are provided at unit or module levels. (C)
_____	_____	_____	4.10	Examples are sequenced from easy to difficult. (C)
_____	_____	_____	4.11	Summaries of content are provided at key break points. (C)
_____	_____	_____	4.12	Humor is used if context may induce fear, tension, or boredom for learners. (C, S)

Applies?	Present?	Rating?		
			5.	**Overt Responses: Program characteristics to stimulate motivated overt learner responses.**
_____	_____	_____	5.1	Requests for meaningful overt learner responses are interspersed within tutorials. (A)
_____	_____	_____	5.2	Program prompts are provided after a designated interval. (A)
_____	_____	_____	5.3	Learner roles are varied through use of role-plays, games, and simulations in addition to tutorial presentations. (A)
_____	_____	_____	5.4	Physical response types (touch screen, keyboard, type-in, capture, reorganize) are varied without causing confusion. (A, C)
_____	_____	_____	5.5	Cognitive response types (select, identify, match, recall, answer, create, etc.) are varied without causing confusion. (A, C)
_____	_____	_____	5.6	Response selections are appropriate for objectives, content, and skills. (R)
_____	_____	_____	5.7	Responses require application of content. (R)
_____	_____	_____	5.8	An opportunity is provided to allow learners to personalize objectives or to add some of their own. (R)
_____	_____	_____	5.9	A variety of instructional resources available (glossary, encyclopedia, expert files, etc.) is available. (C)
_____	_____	_____	5.10	Directions are simple and clear. (C)
_____	_____	_____	5.11	Adequate time is allowed for learner response. (C)
_____	_____	_____	5.12	Practice examples are sequenced from easy to difficult. (C)
_____	_____	_____	5.13	Learners are given at least two chances to respond to practice items. (C)
_____	_____	_____	5.14	Appropriate tangible "takeaways" are provided such as job aids, handouts, certificates, etc. (S)
_____	_____	_____	5.15	The number of examples and practice exercises are appropriate for the learners. (C, S)
			6.	**Feedback. Program characteristics to sustain motivation through feedback.**
_____	_____	_____	6.1	Feedback is appropriate for learner characteristics. (A)
_____	_____	_____	6.2	Feedback style varies without causing confusion. (A)
_____	_____	_____	6.3	Feedback relates practice exercises to job or real-life applications when appropriate. (R)
_____	_____	_____	6.4	Corrective feedback focuses on tasks and content, not on personal traits of learners. (C)
_____	_____	_____	6.5	Confirming feedback is used to reinforce correct answers. (C)

Applies?	Present?	Rating?		
_____	_____	_____	6.6	Knowledge of results (KOR) is provided for drill and practice. (C)
_____	_____	_____	6.7	KOR plus correct answers are provided where problem types or difficulty levels vary. (C)
_____	_____	_____	6.8	KOR, correct answers, and rationale are provided for evaluative, analytical or synthesis practices. (C)
_____	_____	_____	6.9	Feedback is provided as soon as possible after practice. (C, S)
_____	_____	_____	6.10	Feedback for simulations show the results of learner decisions as realistically as possible. (R)
_____	_____	_____	6.11	Clues are provided after wrong responses for content that is complex, or for learners for whom the content is difficult. (C)
_____	_____	_____	6.12	Appropriate review and/or new study is recommended or required for remediation. (C)
_____	_____	_____	6.13	Level of feedback (KOR, correct answers, rationale, remediation) is appropriate for objectives and content. (C)

Reference

For information on the ARCS model and its application to software design, see Keller, J. M. & Suzuki, K. (1988). Use of the ARCS motivation model in courseware design. In Jonassen, D. H. (Ed), *Instructional designs for microcomputer courseware.* Hillsdale N.J.: Lawrence Erlbaum Associates.

This checklist contains 49 questions to aid you in the selection of multimedia software that will motivate your students. Even the most exciting software can become boring when the novelty expires.

Summary

In summary, hypermedia-authoring systems offer teachers the most flexible means to create individualized lesson plans for their students. However, the development of such lessons requires time and knowledge of an authoring system. You may recall that, when computers first became available, many researchers indicated that teachers needed to begin to develop their own CAI software. Hindsight indicates that teachers did not need "programming" skills because the commercial market provided most of the early CAI packages. In short, the suggestions that indicate that teachers should plan to develop hypermedia stacks may seem similar to the earlier aborted attempts to encourage all teachers to become programmers.

However, there are several differences. First, the authoring programs currently available for developing hypermedia are much more user friendly than the earlier programming languages with which teachers had to contend. Also, since many hypermedia stacks already exist, the current authoring systems may be used merely to link informational stacks that already exist. This process is simpler than writing the detailed program statements that were required in earlier CAI development. For these reasons, it seems likely that many more teachers will learn to develop hypermedia stacks than were involved in earlier versions of CAI programming. The use of prepared stacks and the courseware-authoring process shown in Figure 6.8 should reduce the time spent and increase the use of these CAI lessons. In the next section, we talk specifically about the multimedia-authoring system *HyperCard*.

If you are familiar with the hypermedia-authoring systems available at your school, you may wish to skip the activity in Try This 6.1.

Try This 6.1
See if your school has any hypermedia-authoring systems. In your search, check for any stacks that have been developed. If you have time, play with this system so you will know what options you have available to you.

HyperCard *by Apple*

HyperCard is one of the most popular programs and provides a good example of a hypermedia-authoring system. The building blocks of *HyperCard* are stacks and objects that include buttons. (Both were described earlier.) The basis of *HyperCard* is five objects: cards, fields, buttons, backgrounds, and stacks (Culp & Watkins, 1995). As mentioned earlier, a card can be thought of as an index card and is a single-screen display. Text or graphics can be displayed on the card, or a card can enable the user to enter text into a text field. A field is an area on a card that can contain text. Fields can have different sizes and the text within the fields can be in different styles, fonts, and sizes. A card can also contain buttons.

As discussed earlier, a button is an area on a card that may be clicked with a mouse or touched with a finger to initiate a specific action that has been programmed in a HyperTalk script. A stack is a collection of cards that contains related information. Background objects are objects that are defined for one or more cards in a series. They provide a means of sharing objects, such as fields and buttons, with several cards. The objects in *HyperCard* may be used to develop stacks that provide nonsequential access to information that may be any combination of text, graphics, video, or sound (Male, 1994; Culp & Watkins, 1995). An example of a card can be found in Figure 6.10.

In addition to objects, *HyperCard* has five user levels that may be set up by the stack user. These levels are browse, type, paint, author, and script.

1. *Browse.* In the browse level, the user can "flip" through cards and stacks, looking for information.
2. *Type.* At the type level, the user can enter or edit text in a field.
3. *Paint.* The paint level allows the user to create graphics for use on cards.
4. *Author.* The author level allows the user to add or remove buttons and fields from cards.
5. *Script.* The script level contains directions to the computer (these directions are written in a language called HyperTalk) to perform certain tasks such as looking at a specific frame of a videodisc, producing a sound effect, and other tasks.

Furthermore, *HyperCard* allows the user to copy scripts from stacks created by others without having to learn HyperTalk. It is common for videodisc producers to publish stackware for use with their laser discs. In particular Apple Computer, Inc., has an Educator's Home Card that contains many useful stacks for teachers. Furthermore, *HyperCard* comes with idea stacks. So

FIGURE 6.10   A Card in HyperCard

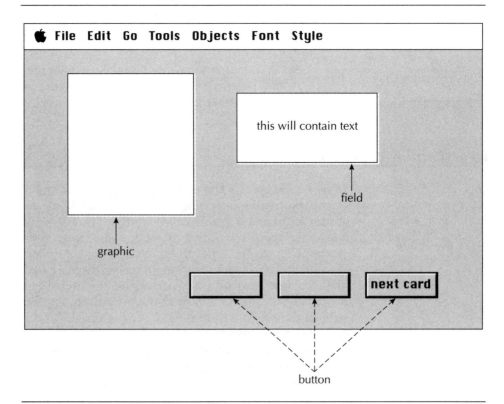

a novice can easily use *HyperCard* by copying and modifying these existing stacks without having to worry about details. Software programs such as *HyperCard* and *Linkway* control devices such as CD-ROM drives and videodisc players so that users may have access to pictures and films in addition to text, graphics, and sound. These packages can be used in two ways: (1) they allow the user to build stacks or applications without knowledge of a programming language and (2) they allow the user to utilize stacks or applications that have been developed by other people.

Figures 6.1 and 6.11 are examples of stacks. Figure 6.1 is an example of a stack put together to give information on St. Augustine, Florida, USA. The four cards shown are a stack. Card 1 has five buttons; clicking on any one of these buttons causes something to happen. Clicking on the button marked Video shows a video of a carriage ride along the harbor of St. Augustine toward a Spanish fort. Clicking on the other four buttons will take the user to another card. Text can be added to a card at the type level of *HyperCard*. The picture of the state of Florida could be drawn by using paint tools or copying and pasting the graphic from a clip-art file. At the browse level, the user can just read the information and move on to other choices.

FIGURE 6.11   Stack from a Multiple-Choice Question

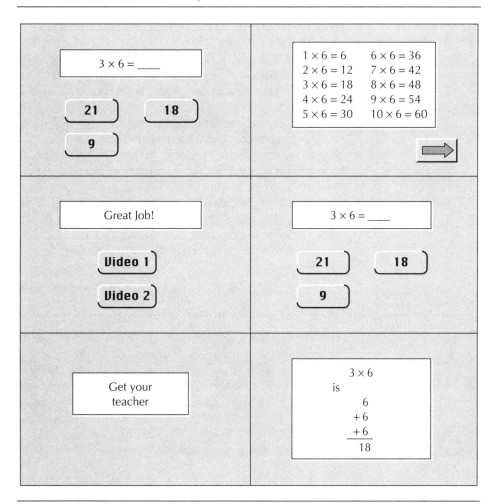

The stack in Figure 6.11 is based on the flowchart for a multiple choice question given in Figure 6.9. The first card presents the questions for the first time with the possible answers as buttons. If the button containing 18 is clicked on, then the next card is the one with reinforcement videos, and the student gets to choose between the two. If the student chooses a wrong answer, then the next card is the 6 times tables, and then the question is shown again. If the student picks a wrong answer again, he or she is shown the card with the text that 3 × 6 is just three 6s added together. Afterward, the student is shown the question again. If the student answers wrong for a third time, he or she is told to get the teacher.

In-Service

Programs such as *HyperCard* and *Linkway* were designed to free programming from computer specialists and make programming options available to the public. In *The Educator's Guide to HyperCard and HyperTalk*, the authors George Culp and Morgan Watkins teach *HyperCard* through the eyes of teachers. Their book, published by Allyn and Bacon, takes teachers through the basics and then goes on to introduce tools that teachers need for working with images, sounds, and hypertext. The examples given in the book focus on applications for teachers. Furthermore, numerous practitioners have used this book in in-service education for teachers (the book includes a course outline for such in-service). Also, the authors provide a five-day in-service for school districts on CAI and multimedia utilization.

There are over 200,000 *HyperCard* stacks that have been developed (Culp & Watkins, 1995). In addition, *HyperCard* gives the teacher the capability to design and develop customized instructional materials. This is particularly important because of the increase in at-risk students in inclusive classrooms.

Proper teacher training is required for technology to be integrated into the learning process. In a guest editorial by Betty Castor (1994), she stated that a survey, done by Bank Street College, indicated that it took five to seven years of training for a teacher to become comfortable and confident in the use of some of the sophisticated education technology. This survey also indicated that it was not until the end of the fifth year that teachers would expand their use of technology beyond drill and practice and tutorial software. In view of this information, we feel that it is essential that the master teacher seek out educational in-service classes on the integration of technology in the classroom.

Future of Multimedia

Another question that master teachers need to ask themselves is: Where do we go from here? Alan D. Morgan, Superintendent of Schools, New Mexico, has an answer in a guest editorial he wrote for the March 1994 issue of *T.H.E. Journal*. In his editorial, Morgan maintains that technology must be used to help develop a management system and a body of learning experiences for students. He identifies five critical components that a fully developed, systemic, technology-based educational system should include. These components are as follows:

1. *A teacher support and information base.* Morgan proposes that this information base match learning resources and techniques to the avail-

able resources. The information base should contain a management system that allows teachers to follow the progress of each student through flexible content standards.

2. *The learning resources themselves.* Morgan feels that these resources will take the form of a virtual digital library. This would be the next technological step after CD-ROMs and videodiscs currently in use.

3. *A communications system.* In the future, each classroom should have direct access to Internet (a worldwide computer network), satellite, and cable communications. These communications should be able to handle text, voice, data, and full-motion video.

4. *Credit to students for out-of-school learning.* Technology should be used to track and assess student activities such as volunteer work and jobs to give them credit for what they have learned.

5. *Assessment.* Technology would allow teachers to keep portfolios of student work, to monitor their progress, and to display their knowledge.

Morgan writes that there are 28 states currently developing plans for the incorporation of technology as a major part of their education reform movements. He feels very strongly that the five components discussed here are the first steps in attaining quality education for every student.

Virtual Reality: Technology of the Future

Now that we have discussed at the current technology, we will project what is around the corner. The next step is virtual reality. Virtual reality is where users interact with computer-generated objects through their body movements. Virtual reality can already be seen in some video games. It allows the user to become an active participant by using gloves, helmets, eye glasses, bodysuits, and chairs. In current video games, users are directors of action rather than participants. In virtual reality, users become active participants.

Bitter, Camuse, and Durbin (1993) feel that virtual reality programs may have educational applications. They predict that students and teachers will go on computer-generated trips and activities that are too costly, dangerous, or unattainable. For example, using virtual reality, students and teachers could experience riding the space shuttle and working in space. Other examples would be to use virtual reality to raft down the Colorado River or explore a rain forest. All of these are trips that are costly and dangerous, but virtual reality can make the experience of these trips possible.

Conclusion

This chapter has discussed the current technology available for classrooms and the technology being developed for the future. As a master teacher, you must not only be current with today's technology but you must also prepare for the future. Preparing for the future includes knowing how multimedia can be used in the classroom and knowing authoring systems such as *HyperCard* or *Linkway*. Clearly, these applications will tend to redesign the traditional classroom, and teachers must be prepared to take a leadership role in their new and challenging electronic environment.

References

Boone, R., Higgins, K., Falba, C., & Langley, W. (1993). Cooperative Text: Reading and Writing in a Hypermedia Environment. *Learning Disabilities Forum*, 19(1), 28–37.

Bitter, G. G., Camuse, R. A., & Durbin, V. L. (1993). *Using a Microcomputer in the Classroom* (3rd ed.). Boston: Allyn and Bacon.

Castor, B. (1994). Guest Editorial. *Technological Horizons in Education Journal*, 21(7), 10.

Culp, G. H., & Watkins, G. M. (1995). *The Educator's Guide to HyperCard and HyperTalk* (revised). Boston: Allyn and Bacon.

Fitzgerald, G. E. (1989). *Authoring Systems for Higher Education*. Postdoctoral training session presented at CEC Project Retool, Long Island University, NY.

Fitzgerald, G. E., Bauder, D. K., & Werner, J. G. (1992). Authoring CAI Lessons: Teachers as Developers. *Teaching Exceptional Children*, 24(2), 15–21.

Gersten, R., Carnine, D., & Woodard, J. (1987). Direct Instruction Research: The Third Decade. *Remedial and Special Education*, 8(6), 48–56.

Hasselbring, T., Sherwood, R., Bransford, J., Fleenor, K., Griffith, D., & Goin, L. (1987). An Evaluation of the Level-One Instructional Videodisc Program. *Journal of Educational Technology Systems*, 16(22), 151–169.

Hofmeister, A. M. (1989). Teaching with Videodiscs. *Teaching Exceptional Children*, 21(3), 52–54.

Hofmeister, A., Engelmann, S., & Carnine, D. (1986). *The Development and Validation of an Instructional Videodisc Program*. Washington, DC: Systems Impact.

Keller, B. H., & Keller, J. M. (1994, March 27). *Meaningful and Motivating Interactivity in Multimedia Instruction: Design and Evaluation Guidelines*. Presented at 11th International Conference on Technologies in Education, London.

Keller, J. M. (1987a). Strategies for Stimulating the Motivation to Learn. *Performance & Instruction*, 26(8), 1–7.

Keller, J. M. (1987b). The Systematic Process of Motivational Design. *Performance & Instruction*, 26(9), 1–8.

Kelly, B., Carnine, D., & Grossen, B. (1986). The Effectiveness of Videodisc Instruction in Teaching Fractions to Learning-disabled and Remedial High School Students. *Journal of Special Education Technology*, 8(2), 5–16.

Lewis, R. B. (1993). *Special Education Technology: Classroom Applications*. Pacific Grove, CA: Brooks/Cole.

Lubke, M. M., Rogers, B., & Evans, K. T. (1989). Teaching Fractions with Videodiscs. *Teaching Exceptional Children*, 21(3), 55–56.

Male, M. (1994). *Technology for Inclusion: Meeting the Special Needs of All Students* (2nd ed.). Boston: Allyn and Bacon.

Meskill, C. (1987). Educational Technology Product Review: Mastering Ratios. *Educational Technology*, 27(7), 41–42.

Miller, S. C., & Cooke, N. L. (1989). Mainstreaming Students with Learning Disabilities for Videodisc Math Instruction. *Teaching Exceptional Children*, 21(3), 57–60.

Monti, D., Cicchetti, G., Goodkind, T., & Ganci, M. (1994). SPT: A New Methodology for Instruction. *Technological Horizons in Education Journal*, 22(1), 66–68.

Morgan, A. D. (1994). Guest Editorial. *Technological Horizons in Education Journal*, 21(8), 10.

Petersen, L., Hofmeister, A., & Lubke, M. (1988). A Videodisc Approach to Instructional Productivity. *Educational Technology*, 28(2), 16–22.

Sampath, S., & Quaine, A. (1990). Effective Interface Tools for CAI Authors. *Journal of Computer-Based Instruction*, 17(1), 31–34.

Steinberg, E. (1984). *Teaching Computers to Teach*. Hillsdale, NJ: Erlbaum.

Wilson, K. (1991). *Bank Street College of Education* (pp. 51–57). Proceedings of the Multimedia Technology Seminar, Washington, DC.

Yarrow, J. (1994). Across the Curriculum with HyperCard. *Technological Horizons in Education Journal*, 21(8), 88–89.

7

Professional Improvement

William N. Bender
Renet L. Bender

Upon completion of this chapter you should be able to:

◆ *Avoid burnout.*

◆ *Implement a professional improvement plan.*

◆ *Acquire grant support for implementation of CAI ideas.*

We have indicated throughout that implementation of CAI can assist a master teacher in totally restructuring the methods of instruction. With some degree of out-of-class work, teachers can employ even the most sophisticated CAI. The payoffs include not only significantly enhanced learning for at-risk students but also more overall enjoyment of teaching for the teacher. Furthermore, CAI use will, in time, reduce the overall workload of the teacher since today it can perform a great deal of individual instruction.

This section looks at several specific ways in which teachers may use CAI to enhance and improve their teaching skills. Unlike the earlier sections of this book, this chapter concentrates on the effects of professional improvement on the master teacher.

What Is Professional Improvement?

Professional improvement encompasses every aspect of a professional's career. However, three general guidelines can serve to enhance professional development throughout one's career. The first involves the enjoyment of teaching, even when feeling somewhat stressed. We present here a number of ideas for constructively handling stress and burnout. Next, one of the most important aspects of personal improvement involves setting yearly goals in order to continue your education throughout your career. This can be achieved through the development of professional improvement plans (called *PIPs*). Finally, a third aspect of professional development involves obtaining money to implement your CAI ideas, in light of tough budgetary periods. The last portion of this chapter elaborates on how to obtain financing for your CAI implementation ideas. In particular, suggestions are offered on how to approach businesses for contributions and/or how to write grants. We hope that this chapter inspires you to improve continually your use of CAI and to develop a yearly plan for self-improvement involving many of these suggestions.

Enjoying Your Teaching

The Burnout Problem

Teaching is a rewarding profession, but with increasing demands on teachers and their role in society, teaching can be a stressful profession. Research has indicated that many teachers may experience burnout. This problem will often surface three to five years after a teacher begins his or her career—the very years at which beginning teachers are reaching the peak of their skills. Clearly, every teacher should be cognizant of this burnout problem. As professionals, you must be aware of the situation and take preventive measures to handle stress constructively and to avoid teacher burnout.

Remedies for Burnout

The following suggestions are provided to help you enjoy your teaching. Many of these suggestions relate directly to CAI use in order to assist you in avoiding burnout (Bender, 1992).

1. Teaching is an ever-evolving profession. Make work exciting by remaining current in professional skills. Read about and practice new instructional techniques, including CAI utilization, on a planned and regular basis. Subscribe to a journal and one or two-teacher oriented magazines, and read them monthly. If you consider yourself a professional, and take actions consistent with that view, you are probably less likely to experience burnout.

2. Attend professional conferences. At the very least, it helps to know that other teachers of at-risk students face the same types of problems. Teachers at these conferences discuss their students and CAI strategies with other conference participants. You may find an idea or two on CAI implementation that you wish to try. Furthermore, other teachers' enthusiasm will help to rejuvenate you.

3. If you are unhappy with your present situation, consider a revitalization in your job by reinventing the way you teach using CAI. One way is to set goals for individual or group CAI instruction and decrease the teaching load with CAI instruction. Another suggestion is to move to another class in the same school district or work with younger/older students. Perhaps moving to another school with different people will help to restructure your teaching to include more CAI.

4. Taking additional coursework in CAI, or other related fields such as counseling, behavior management, behavioral disorders, or early childhood education, will help to rejuvenate you. As a student, you will be introduced to new CAI teaching methods and will be able to talk about your work with other teachers.

5. Consider supervising a student teacher. Nothing is more exciting than contributing to the training of a new teacher. You can, with the student teacher, explore various new CAI applications. This is a chance to share your

experiences and knowledge gained throughout years of teaching, as well as to profit from the newer techniques that a student teacher can share.

6. Teach, on an adjunct basis, a college-level class for pre-service teachers. With this type of teaching, you will be exposed to the newest research, have a chance to talk with college faculty in education, and teach college students.

7. Design and conduct CAI research with faculty from a local college or university that is intended to rectify a problem you face in your class. When you work on rectifying a problem, and succeed, you will have a sense of accomplishment.

8. When you find you have feelings of burnout, talk about these feelings with other teachers and elicit ideas they use to avoid burnout. Sometimes attending a conference and talking with peers can be the best solution when you are feeling this way.

9. It is often helpful to contact students whom you taught in the past and find out what types of instruction they felt was most helpful. Use this information to modify your professional goals.

10. When you are feeling burnout, take responsibility for your own feelings and work in some fashion to alleviate those feelings. Do not ignore these feelings; they will not go away on their own. It is up to you, the master teacher, to take some initiative to deal with these feelings.

11. Talk with your current students about what they would like to do in class. Find out what types of CAI they consider to be fun and incorporate these ideas into your lessons.

In summary, take responsibility for your own feelings. Work at developing a good working environment in your school and classroom. You will be happier when you are striving for tough professional improvement goals.

Personal Improvement

Improving your skills and abilities with each succeeding year in the profession should be one goal of every master teacher. Setting a goal for personal improvement can assist in the prevention of burnout (as just discussed). Beginning teachers are learning and practicing the skills of teaching during the first several years, but more experienced teachers—master teachers—have already developed their professional skills and classroom management style. These master teachers then are free to concentrate on more refined instructional techniques, such as increasing effective use of CAI in their classrooms. To illustrate this type of "master teacher" professionalism, consider the following questions: Who would want to go to a doctor who last participated in any medical training over 25 years ago? What would be the level of care provided by that physician? Would you wish to retain an attorney who had not remained current in his or her awareness of recent case law and legal strategy? More pointedly, do you wish to send your children to a teacher who had his or her most recent training 10, 15, or 20 years ago, with only a few subsequent in-service credits?

As these questions illustrate, master teachers should make a yearly effort to remain current in their professional field. This responsibility is part of the definition of professionalism. Most states require periodic courses for recertification, and this is certainly a fundamental step in the right direction. However, teachers in such states should not assume that such minimal coursework every third or fifth year is enough. As this text indicates, CAI use has changed radically since the early days of "drill and practice" CAI programs. Further, those so-called early days were less than a decade ago. Teachers who take their professional responsibilities seriously will go much further than the recertification requirements in order to keep up with the rapid change in areas such as CAI instruction.

One method for professional improvement is the creation of a written agreement between a teacher and his or her supervisor or principal that specifies a set of professional activities in which the teacher will engage during the coming year. Some states and school districts have taken the positive step of requiring such documentation of professional improvement from each teacher. Various school districts in New Jersey, West Virginia, and numerous other states have implemented this requirement.

The *professional improvement plan (PIP)* (Bender, 1992) is a document that represents the agreement between a teacher and a school district. Generally, it specifies the activities in which a teacher will engage during the following year in order to improve his or her teaching performance. Of course, the PIP should involve activities in numerous areas of education, and not merely CAI. However, for our purposes, we will specify the PIP in terms of professional development in use and applications of CAI, as discussed in this book.

The range of activities appropriate for the PIP is almost endless. Activities such as reading CAI research articles, participating in presentations or in-service classes regarding CAI, implementing new teaching techniques utilizing CAI, completing additional coursework from universities, creating annotated bibliographies, conducting CAI research, observing the use of CAI in other classes, serving as mentor teacher to new teachers setting up CAI, and many other activities are appropriate for the PIP. Almost any activity that encourages either more effective CAI or more awareness of recent CAI research in the field would be appropriate. Figure 7.1 is one example of a PIP.

Such professional improvement planning may be more necessary in the field of special education than in other areas. This field has existed for only 30 years—a brief history compared to other areas such as research on elementary education or secondary subject area training. Clearly, special education is one area in which teachers will want to remain current on the CAI research.

Figure 7.1 Professional Improvement Plan

Goal 1. Work toward recertification
Objective 1. Take one course on CAI from a local college.
Objective 2. Submit course outline to state certification office.

Goal 2. Increase the use of CAI in the classroom
Objective 1. Complete two CAI software evaluations, each of which will include a research and an applications evaluation of the software.
Objective 2. Attend a half-day in-service class on CAI.
Objective 3. Prepare documentation to request contributions from local businesses for CAI software.

Goal 3. Professional visibility
Objective 1. Present a paper on CAI applications at an in-state professional conference.
Objective 2. Conduct a 1.5-hour workshop on CAI applications for the school faculty.

What does it mean to be involved with research? This question can be answered with three mandates: Read CAI research, implement CAI in your curricula, and conduct CAI research (Bender, 1992). In addition to participating in research, teachers can do other activities such as software evaluations, participate in classes and in-service, and serve on state, local, and professional committees to attain personal improvement goals. Each of these options is discussed here.

Reading CAI Research

Reading about CAI research can help teachers decide which CAI software to use in their classroom. The literature contains numerous articles on the selection of CAI software, and the integration of CAI software in classrooms. Some articles even contain reviews of particular CAI packages.

CAI is a constantly evolving area. Therefore, teachers of at-risk students should read several CAI articles monthly that come directly from the major journals in their field. Although articles from teacher magazines may provide information on a new idea involving CAI for your class, the only manner in which a you may remain current with research is to subscribe to and regularly read one of the major journals in your field. *The Journal of Special Education, Learning Disability Quarterly, Mental Retardation,* and *Remedial and Special Education,* are all major journals that are highly regarded and that regularly include articles on CAI use in the classroom. Other journals that have articles relating to at-risk students or CAI technology and use include *Exceptional Children, Psychology in the Schools, The Journal of Special Education Technology, Conn SENSE Bulletin, Closing the Gap,* and *Teaching Exceptional Children.* Also, subscriptions for some of these journals is included in membership of certain organizations. For example, by joining the Council for Exceptional Children (CEC), you will receive two of these journals. By joining the Technology and Media Division of CEC, you receive one of the journals mentioned and a newsletter specifically designed to meet the needs of teachers using technology.

It is difficult to imagine a physician who does not subscribe to at least one medical journal or an attorney who does not order at least one law journal, yet it is quite common for teachers who have finished their training to stop subscribing to the major journals in the field. Do not accept such a low professional standard for yourself. Make a point of reading at least one journal article each month in order to remain current in your profession. *Technological Horizons in Education Journal* is one journal on technological innovations that we have found particularly helpful. Subscriptions to this journal are free or under $35, depending on the subscribing organization.

In order to document these reading efforts for the PIP, you may need to prepare an annotated bibliography of the articles or a brief synopsis of each article. Requirements for reviewing 10 to 15 articles during a school year are not uncommon, and that reading requirement is consistent with the workload of a master teacher.

If you wish to talk to others about CAI and professional development, the activity in Try This 7.1 offers some suggestions.

> ***Try This 7.1*** *Form a CAI interest group with a few colleagues for purposes of subscribing to journals and developing a dialog on CAI usage. Have each person in the group subscribe to a different journal and share that journal and any applicable CAI arti-*

cles with the group. The group may also wish to share annotated bibliographies of articles that individual members have read. We have seen interest groups such as this grow to become influential in the local school and/or school district discussion regarding CAI implementation.

Implementing CAI Curricula

As teacher trainers, we have often seen teachers who read about a new idea for CAI in a journal then apply it in their own classroom. For example, in our classes, we have seen teachers study and integrate word processing in their curricula merely because they read about it in a journal. This type of initiative seems to characterize the most effective teachers of at-risk students. These teachers seem always willing to attempt a new idea in order to improve their teaching for the students in their classes.

The challenge for you is clear: It is your task to read and implement new ideas for CAI in your classroom on a periodic basis. Perhaps a good goal would be to apply at least one new CAI teaching package during every two months of teaching. In that fashion, you will at least experiment with approximately 10 new CAI techniques during the first two years in the classroom. You may then choose to retain the ones that work and forgo use of the ones that do not seem applicable in your situation.

Documentation of the use of these new CAI teaching packages in your classroom may be necessary for the PIP, and such documentation may be handled in several ways. One goal for the PIP would involve development of software evaluations for two or three of these packages. These could be submitted to the principal and placed in the media center for use by others as a part of your PIP. Next, you may produce some type of presentation for faculty concerning these packages, complete with information that documents their effectiveness. Another option is to invite the principal or supervisor to observe you while you engage in using the new package or instructional method. Then that supervisor could write a brief report of the activity for your PIP documentation.

Conducting CAI Research

Most of the CAI research that is published in journals is conducted by university and college faculty, and some is conducted by public school administrators and supervisors. Only rarely does one see an article in which a classroom teacher conducts CAI research. Nevertheless, teachers should frequently conduct CAI research—though in order to fully understand this injunction, the definition of research may need to be expanded.

Within the national movement for school reform, proponents of reform have begun to use the term *action research* to focus on the teachers' responsibility to conduct research that is directly related to the actions of teaching in the classroom. For example, if a teacher notes a writing deficiency and then successfully integrates word processing to help his or her at-risk students write better, that may be considered action-based research in some sense. In that example, a problem was noted and measured, a hypothesis was stated, an intervention was implemented, and research was conducted to validate the intervention. The results could then be shared with parents, school psychologists, and other teachers in order to communicate about the problem and its elimination.

All teachers of at-risk students should find ample opportunities to participate in action research on CAI in their classes. The usefulness of CAI research such as this is not dependent on publication in the professional journals. Rather, the focus of such research is improvement in teaching. Also, when you share successful CAI research with parents and other professionals, you gain respect in their eyes, and that is one worthy goal of such action-based research. Conducting research of this nature and sharing the results will contribute to a positive professional reputation for you.

In many instances, teachers have conducted action research projects on CAI in which the quality and general instructiveness of the finished product warranted publication in the journals. When a teacher demonstrates the effectiveness of a new CAI idea or merely modifies an old idea, the teacher should be encouraged to publish that action research, if possible. Generally, such teachers find it helpful to work with someone who has publication experience in their efforts to publish research results. Still, if a teacher modifies a CAI idea from the journals and demonstrates its effectiveness, he or she should consider publication. This desire to share effective CAI strategies is one mark of a professional teacher.

A final option that should be explored is participation in ongoing CAI research in your school district. For example, many school districts encourage college and university faculty to conduct research in the public school classes for at-risk students, because this serves to keep public school faculties more current in research. This usually involves some degree of time commitment to the research, and you will wish to weigh that time commitment against the positive gains for yourself and for the school district. In many instances, researchers will return to the district after the research is concluded and share the results with the faculty involved. Also, there may be individual publication possibilities for you in particular research projects. Finally, when possible, all teachers of at-risk students should encourage and participate in CAI research if the knowledge of these students and methods of instruction is to continue to grow.

Documentation of research participation on the PIP is fairly straightforward. First, if you participate in an ongoing research project at your school, this may be stipulated in the original PIP agreement at the beginning of the school year. Next, if you find that a particular CAI project is beneficial during the year, you may amend your PIP in order to include that project when it is completed.

In one instance, we have seen PIPs for supervisory personnel in a school district that require publications of articles in major journals. Such a requirement may be overly ambitious—indeed, it may be quite excessive for teachers. However, the field of education could only be improved if public school personnel took a more active hand in providing substantive literature in the field. This would serve to keep research, overall, from becoming too theoretical, and would provide reality-based research for the field. If you publish a paper in one of the journals or teacher magazines, you should amend your PIP during that year to include that accomplishment.

Of course, another option for dissemination of action research on CAI involves presentations at professional meetings. Teachers should be encouraged to present the results of their action research to others in forums of this nature, and that accomplishment should be noted on the PIP.

Software Evaluations

Part of being a master teacher is performing software evaluations. These evaluations include research and applications evaluations that are an integral part in the selection of CAI software for your classroom. Both types of evaluations are discussed in Chapter 3 and should be included in your PIP. You should use both of these types of evaluations in building a file for your school or district of CAI software evaluations. Furthermore, if there is a local publication (perhaps a local CAI interest group newsletter), you should consider publishing the software evaluations you conduct in that newsletter. When performing applications evaluations for a central file, you may wish to include a paragraph with suggestions for using the CAI software and the appropriate skill level of students for the package. Each person using the package or testing it on his or her students could then add personal comments to the evaluation.

Participation in Classes and In-Service

Many PIPs specify that teachers will participate in various workshops, in-service meetings, and college-level classes. For example, if you have noted a problem in integrating CAI in your classroom, you may wish to participate in a three-day workshop on CAI integration. Documentation of these activities would be provided merely by attendance records.

Many teachers who choose not to publish results of their work do share their innovative ideas by presenting various workshops and in-service sessions at state, regional, or national meetings. For example, the national meeting of the Council for Exceptional Children has numerous presentation forums in which teachers share their innovative ideas with other teachers. Documentation of attendance and presentations at meetings such as these should certainly be included in the PIP.

Serving on State, Local, and Professional Committees

In the area of integration of CAI in the classroom, a great deal of work remains to be done. At times, state or local education agencies will form working committees to deal with issues regarding CAI, purchasing of computers, software selection, and many other tasks. Likewise, many of the organizations concerned with at-risk students (e.g., Council for Learning Disabilities, Council for Exceptional Children) have committees that debate professional issues within the field. Service on such working committees is another professional activity that can improve your professional skills. For the PIP, documentation of work on these types of committees can usually be handled by a letter from the committee chairperson.

Summary of Professional Improvement

The educational opportunities for at-risk students will continue to improve only if the professional preparedness of the teachers of these students continues to improve. Therefore, it is the responsibility of each master teacher of at-risk students to set goals, at least on a yearly basis, and conduct activities that may improve his or her abilities and skills with these students. Certainly constant improvement in CAI applications should be included on every master teacher's PIP.

While some states and school districts require PIPs from each professional, there is no reason why teachers in other districts should not use a PIP to stipulate their own goals for professional improvement. Even in districts where PIPs are not required, many principals would be very pleased to see individual teachers who set and attain goals on a yearly basis that are consistent with professional improvement. Such goal setting can indicate your desire to be the most effective professional you can be. As a master teacher, after the first few years of teaching are over, you may wish to consider devising a PIP and sharing it with your supervisor and principal. That individual would then be able to give you guidance and feedback concerning your intended improvement areas, and such participation would indicate to him or her your willingness to learn. If you have written a PIP, you may wish to skip the activity in Try This 7.2.

> **Try This 7.2**   *Using Figure 7.1 as a model, write your own PIP. Be careful not to overextend yourself.*

Obtaining Money and Support for Your CAI Implementation Ideas

When there is some equipment or software that you feel would benefit your students that the school system cannot afford, you should explore other options for obtaining those funds. You may wish to request contributions from various sources or you may consider writing a grant for those funds. Funds from these sources will allow you to stretch your local school budget and to fund long-term projects. Money for funding your projects can come from many sources, including federal funds, state funds, private donations, foundations, local businesses, and local fund-raising activities. Figure 7.2 contains several funding sources from *T.H.E. Journal* that you may wish to examine (Zimet, 1993).

FIGURE 7.2   Grant Resource List

Education Week
P.O. Box 2083
Marion, OH 43306–2183
(800) 346–1834

Federal Register
(202) 708–8773

Major Resource Directories

Education Funding Research Council
(800) 876–0226

Capitol Publishers
(800) 221–0425

Foundation Directories

Foundation Reporter Corporate Giving Directory
(800) 877–8238

The Foundation Grants Index
(800) 424–9836

Funding Update Subscription Service

Education Resources Forecast by Date
Marcella Sherman
(408) 258–8020

Approaching Businesses and Local Organizations

There are various community organizations that support charitable causes, including education. These groups may include organizations such as the Moose, the Rotary, various church groups, and Jewish organizations. In addition to community organizations, many businesses will also support schools with donations of money, new or used computers, or software.

Donations are not automatic, however, and you should approach businesses for donations in a professional way. For example, at a minimum, you should have documentation from your school authorizing you to solicit donations for the school, and a brief description of the particular project you have in mind.

When approaching businesses and organizations, a letter of introduction from your principle on school letterhead, such as the one presented in Figure 7.3, will greatly enhance your efforts. Note that the letter stresses effective financial management for the project. Also, the letter indicates that the project seems to have a good chance of success. This will let the potential donor know that the money or donation will be used for the intended purpose and will be well spent.

You should also take with you a one-page description of your project that clearly states your needs and budget. An example of a project description, including a budget, can be seen in Figure 7.4.

FIGURE 7.3 *Sample Letter of Introduction*

Oconee Junior High School
1285 Cedar Road
Pollocksville, NC 30634

January 14, 1995

To whom it may concern:

Ms. Marie Smith LaFleur is a teacher at our school. She has developed a very good project idea for our students, but she is in need of funding for the project. This project is intended for use with at-risk students and students with disabilities. As you know, students with disabilities have difficulties in various curriculum areas. I believe that this project can greatly enhance our efforts for the at-risk students in our class.

Any funds given for the purpose of the project will be administered by my office, solely for the project proposed herein. I hope that you will give her project consideration. Thank you for meeting with her, and we appreciate your support.

Sincerely,

Mr. Bob Clement
Principal
Oconee Junior High School

FIGURE 7.4   Sample Project Description

Word-Processing Project
Oconee Junior High School

Ms. Marie Smith LaFleur

At-risk students typically require more time and practice to master skills and learn material. Also, writing assignments can be particularly difficult for them. The goal of this project is to provide these students with word-processing experience in their studies and prepare them for jobs once they leave school.

These students, who will benefit from this project, range in grade from seventh to ninth. Most of these students have completed an initial typing class, but they need more practice to enhance their writing skills. At this time, students are ready to learn word-processing software that is useful in business and industry. I feel that learning and using a professional word-processing package such as WordPerfect and/or Microsoft Word will tremendously benefit these students. I plan to require two written assignments each week to be done on a word-processing package.

This school has a typing teacher, so the implementation of this project will be done with the support of this teacher and the vocational technology teacher.

Needs and Budget:
2 new computers	$2,000 for both
2 word-processing packages	$ 300 for both

Total funding required to implement this project is $2,300.

Armed with the preceding information, you may approach small businesses yourself. You may wish to call and make an appointment with the president or manager, or you may simply try dropping in during business hours. In approaching local community organizations, you may wish to do so through a member or officer of the organization.

Local businesses and organizations are an excellent way to implement smaller projects. Approaching these groups requires substantially less paperwork than grants (see next section) and encourages local involvement in community schools.

Grant Writing

Grant writing encompasses proposals submitted for federal, state, foundation, and/or corporation grants. These proposals can range from 2 typed pages to well over 100 pages, but guidelines are available to help you in writing these proposals (Zimet, 1993).

Federal and state grants usually require a multipage proposal that must include district and local documentation pages. Foundations and corporate funding generally require shorter proposals, and may include only a cover letter, a 2- to 10-page project description, along with tax or budget information. No matter where you seek additional funding, everyone will want to know who you are, what the problems are, and what you will do with the money once you receive the funds. In that sense, the basic information you developed for soliciting local contributions must be included in an extended form for larger grant projects. Figure 7.5 at the end of this chapter is an example of a small grant that was written by a master teacher.

The RFP

Most funding sources have a predetermined philosophical idea of the programs and projects they are willing to fund (Zimet, 1993). The funding source will also instruct you in the procedure it wants you to follow before awarding the money. Typically, the philosophical intent and outline for applying for funds is outlined in a document referred to as a *Request for Proposals,* or *RFP.* The RFP will also include all the relevant forms that the organization will require. You should make sure that your project meets the requirements as outlined in the RFP of the funding source. Also, your proposal should include strong qualitative and quantitative data for the project. In general, a grant proposal should cover three topics:

1. The proposal should explain the problems at the school.
2. The proposal should offer ideas on how to solve these problems.
3. The proposal should provide plans on how the solution will be achieved, including necessary costs and personnel required (Zimet, 1993).

Care should be taken in writing the grant proposal to clearly explain the needs of the students and the willingness of the school to change education in terms of at-risk student needs. Strict adherence to the requirements in the RFP is essential. Remember that a large number of other applicants will be seeking support for other projects, and good project ideas are frequently eliminated because the procedures stipulated in the RFP were not followed exactly.

Phases in Grant Preparation

Grants can be individual or group projects. This section discusses group grant writing. When a group of people are going to write a grant, Zimet (1993) suggests that this process be separated into four general phases:

1. Start a committee of several people charged with developing a list of your school's current resources and programs. The goal of this committee is to produce a list of potential projects or project suggestions for the grant. Furthermore, this list will demonstrate your school's ability to manage resources and programs. Have the committee identify situations at your school that require change, and projects that initiate that change.
2. Start a data committee to gather data to support your claims. The needs of your school, delineated in your proposal, must be supported by good measurable data.
3. You should develop a clear vision of what it is you want to accomplish to address these needs. Furthermore, this vision must be shared by the majority of people in your school that will be involved with the project. Your vision should include reasons why funding would be necessary.
4. The writing of the grant can be done by several people, but one person should rewrite the entire proposal so that the grant proposal will have one voice. In writing the grant proposal, you will need to double-check that the needs stipulated in the grant match with the RFP for the chosen source of funding.

Grant Enhancement Suggestions

After you have checked your funding source and established that your needs meet the requirements, the rest of the proposal will consist of the following points for each identified need. Each need should have:

1. An activity addressing the identified need
2. A measurable objective
3. The ability to evaluate the activity based on the objective
4. A reasonable timeline that meets the funding source's program
5. A budget that pays for the established activities
6. Responsible, experienced personnel to carry out the program

Zimet (1993) gives a few further suggestions for writing grant proposals:

1. Read the Request for Proposals (RFP) sent by the funding source carefully and follow all directions.
2. Answer all questions in the RFP in the order they are asked while trying to present as soon as possible what it is you are trying to achieve.
3. Have several teachers read your grant before submitting it. Have the severest critics read your proposal several times as you revise it. Your proposal must be clear, concise, and the best product you can produce. If possible, have someone review the grant who has submitted grants before.
4. Make your proposal easy to read by refraining from the use of jargon. It should be written on a reasonable reading level.
5. Be sensitive to readers' potential concerns. Watch gender, ethnicity, and socioeconomic or educational status references in your proposal.
6. Your final grant proposal should present a professional image with no spelling or grammatical errors. Triple-check your finished written product, and get someone else to check it, before submitting it.

Summary

When a project in your school needs funding outside of the school system, there are several alternatives for funding. These include local businesses and organizations and grants. Approaching local businesses and organizations should be done personally and you should give to them a letter of introduction and a one-page description of your project, including budget. For example, you might first approach a computer store about possibly donating two word-processing packages to the school. The computer store may then be able to provide information about other businesses that are updating their computer systems and will have used computers that may be donated to the schools.

Another means to provide funding for larger or long-term projects is by obtaining a grant. Grants may include federal, state, foundation, and corporate funding sources. These proposals may range from 2 to 100 pages and should strictly adhere to the RFP.

Conclusion

In this chapter, we have discussed professional improvement and the avoidance of burnout. In particular, we advocated a Professional Improvement Plan for every teacher. In your PIP, we recommended including reading CAI research, implementing CAI curricula, and conducting CAI research.

Obtaining support for your CAI ideas was also discussed. The two avenues that teachers have available to them for outside funding are to approach businesses and local organizations, and to apply for grants. Suggestions for approaching outside sources of funding were given.

References

Bender, W. N. (1992). *Learning Disabilities, Characteristics Identification and Teaching Strategies*. Boston: Allyn and Bacon.

Zimet, E. (1993). Grant Writing Techniques for K–12 Funding. *Technological Horizons in Education Journal*, 21(4), 109–112.

FIGURE 7.5 *Sample Grant Application*

SOUTH CAROLINA DEPARTMENT OF EDUCATION
BLOCK GRANT SECTION

EIA COMPETITIVE TEACHER GRANT APPLICATION

SECTION I — General Information

Submit an original and three (3) copies of this project to the Department of Education.

School District Name Oconee County	Project Number (Leave blank)

Person to whom correspondence should be directed in regard to this application.

Name Elizabeth W. Edmondson   Position Science Teacher
Name of School West-Oak High School
Street Address of School Route 5, Box 206
City and Zip Code of School Westminster   29693
Telephone Number of School 647-2018

Project Title (Not more than 5 words) DNA Fingerprinting in the Classroom

Number of Participating Teachers One

Grade Levels Participating 10th

Number of Schools Participating One

Check One: (X) Single-year application   ( ) Multi-year application

Grant Period: From July 1, 1990   to June 30, 1991

Teacher Grant Funds Requested (in whole dollars) $2000.00

Project Category (Check only one)

_____	Social Studies	_____	Gifted and Talented
_____	Reading	_____	Guidance
X	Science	_____	Compensatory Education
_____	Music	_____	Library/Media Services
_____	Language Arts	_____	Special Education
_____	Math	_____	Other (Indicate Area _____)

Continued

SECTION II — Assurances

A.   I do hereby certify that all of the information, figures, and representations made in this application are true and correct to the best of my knowledge and belief. I further certify that the educational program proposed will be carried out to the best of my ability if the application is approved.

       I understand that if any copyrightable material is developed in the course of this grant, the South Carolina Department of Education shall have royalty-free, non-exclusive and irrevocable right to reproduce, publish, or otherwise use and to authorize others to use the work for South Carolina Department of Education purposes.

Date _____ Signature _____
Applicant

B.   I, the principal of the school in which the applicant teacher is employed, am aware of the program outlined in the application, approve of it, and will help achieve the objectives of the program.

Date _____ Signature _____
Principal

C.   I, the Superintendent of the LEA in which the applicant teacher's school is located, am aware of the program outlined in the attached application and agree to receive the funds if the application is approved, to pay out the funds upon written request of the applicant teacher, and to account for the funds as in a special school account. I further agree that these funds will be used only as prescribed by the applicant teacher in reaching the objectives of the proposal. All expenditures of funds received under this grant will be audited by a certified public accountant as a part of the district's annual audit.

Date _____ Signature _____
Superintendent

SECTION III — Project Summary

DNA Fingerprinting, an advanced biotechnology, will provide vocational/technical students in Biology courses with a hands-on application to increase their achievement and understanding of the relationship between science, technology, and society in their genetics unit. Industries using this technology need students with greater technical skills and higher levels of understanding. These needs are not being met by Biology classes at this time as evidenced by science CTBS scores. Surveyed students indicated that the Biology texts do not provide the students with applications of interest or the hands-on experience they obtain in vocational courses. If this grant is funded, these needs will be addressed in hands-on laboratory experiments, a library research project, demonstrations, speakers, Genetic Engineering Filmstrips, and lecture. This approach to understanding genetics will have been successful if the assessment procedures for each objective are successfully completed by 75% of the students involved.

SECTION IV — Problem Area

West-Oak High School is set in a rural community with 790 students in grades 9 through 12. The goal and objectives of this grant are designed to provide vocational/technical track students (51% of West-Oak's student population) with a relevant application, DNA Fingerprinting, and hands-on experience with biotechnology in the genetics unit of Practical Biology (10th grade science course).

Research shows that vocational/technical completers do not have the skills necessary to meet the needs of our technologically advanced industries (U.S. News and World Report, 6/26/89; Fortune, 6/19/89). DNA Fingerprinting and similar technologies require that students understand complex concepts related to genetics and develop advanced laboratory skills. The biology courses these students enroll in test concepts at a lower level than for students in college-preparatory classes and develop fewer laboratory skills. This does not provide them with skills necessary to work in industries using biotechnology. In addition, the science CTBS percentile scores at West-Oak (11th graders in 1989 scored at the 56.4 percentile with a state percentile of 48.4) reflect an incomplete understanding of science topics. The advanced skills and understanding required by biotechnology industries will not be met based on West-Oak's scores. Students must develop a more complete understanding of science concepts to be beneficial to the biotechnology industry.

Research on vocational completers has shown that they learn best through applications and hands-on experience (Center for Occupational Research and Development). A survey of my students showed that 95% of them felt their text was not relevant to their personal needs and career goals. They also felt that the text did not provide the hands-on experiences that they receive in vocational courses. Finally, this technology is not dealt with in the traditional vocational programs thus limiting students possible career choices.

SECTION V — Statement of Goals and Objectives

If West-Oak High School is awarded this grant, the overall goal of this program will be to increase achievement and improve the ability of vocational/technical students to comprehend and analyze the relationship between science, technology, and society in genetics by introducing the technology of DNA Fingerprinting.

Specific objectives of the grant proposal will be:
A — Identification of sources of DNA for producing DNA Fingerprints.
B — Describing a procedure for extracting DNA from cells.
C — Identification of materials and equipment used to carry out a DNA Fingerprint.
D — Analysis of actual DNA Fingerprints to learn how science and technology are used by society.
E — Researching one of the uses of DNA Fingerprints (i.e. rape and homicide cases) and accessing the societal implications of using these fingerprints.
F — Identification of two possible careers using the technology of DNA Fingerprinting.

Continued

SECTION VI — Evaluation Plan

A formal assessment of objective:

A will be the correct identification of at least 4 sources of DNA for Fingerprints by 75% of the students involved.

B will be done by teacher evaluation of an essay. In it, the student must describe correctly at least two of the steps used in DNA extraction.

C will be done by teacher evaluation of a formal laboratory report describing their overall findings with answers to several application questions. On a written test, 75% of the students involved will identify the materials and equipment used, describe how materials (such as: restriction enzymes) and the equipment perform their jobs, and list the possible results that may be obtained.

D will have 75% of the students involved examine and draw conclusions correctly based on the evidence provided in two fingerprints.

E will be done by teacher evaluation of their research papers and class presentations. In these, students must include a thorough explanation of one use of DNA Fingerprinting with two possible costs and benefits to society for mastery.

F will be done by teacher evaluation of an essay. In it, the student must describe one possible career and two tasks carried out by that employee successfully for mastery.

SECTION VII — Description of Activities

Activities for Objective:

A — Students will learn about the sources of DNA for Fingerprinting through reading articles that discuss DNA Fingerprinting and a class lecture.

B — Students will observe a demonstration that will show one method for extracting DNA. This demonstration will obtain DNA from the testis of a cow.

C — Students will carry out a laboratory experiment, using the DNA Restriction Analysis Kit, which will introduce them to the materials, equipment, and steps in producing a DNA Fingerprint. Students will view a filmstrip titled Changing Genetic Messages.

D — Students will carry out a laboratory experiment that will produce a simulated DNA Fingerprint. They will analyze the fingerprint they produce to determine similarities in patterns. They will also work with drawings of simulated fingerprints from rape, homicide, and maternity-paternity cases obtained from science articles. They will work with a photograph of a fingerprint from 14 peach varieties obtained from Dr. Abbott's DNA Fingerprinting Research Lab at Clemson.

E — Students will research a use of DNA Fingerprinting (such as: rape and homicide cases, maternity-paternity cases, cultivar identification, and big-game forensics—prevention of elephant poaching) and its societal implications in our library. Societal implications will be addressed by students determining the costs and benefits to society. They will write a paper reporting their findings and conclusions and make a 5 to 10 minute presentation. Students will also view a filmstrip titled Issues in Genetic Engineering.

F — Two speakers will present their work with DNA Fingerprinting. The first speaker, Lorri Medlin, will represent the Forensics Lab at SLED in Columbia. She will describe how DNA Fingerprinting is being used there. The second speaker, Linda Eldredge, is a research technician in Dr. Abbott's DNA Fingerprinting Research Facility at Clemson. I invited Ms. Eldredge because of her skills as a technician and the role model she provides for students.

SECTION VIII — Time Line

September 1, 1990	— Supplies and Materials will be ordered.
November 5, 1990	— Confirm 2 DNA Fingerprinting speakers for the Genetics unit.
February 4, 1991	— Genetics unit will start.
March 6, 1991	— Genetics unit will be completed.
May 1, 1991	— Exportable Product Completed.
May 15, 1991	— Final Report Completed and Mailed to the State Department.

SECTION IX — Exportable Product Description

If awarded this grant, I will develop a booklet for teachers describing the project.
This booklet will include:

a) The Goal, Objectives, and Needs addressed by this project.
b) Schedule of topics addressed with a brief description of each day.
c) Lab Procedures for teachers, an equipment and materials list, possible vendors, and expected results.
d) Lab Handouts for students.
e) Worksheets for students viewing the Genetic Engineering Filmstrips.
f) Research Paper topics with a description of how students should access the costs and benefits to society.
g) Simulated DNA Fingerprints for students to analyze.
h) Notes on Speaker Presentations.
i) Reference List

I will also present the exportable product at the 1991 South Carolina Science Teachers Convention.

Continued

SECTION X — Budget Breakdown

The categories for expenditures are grouped below by "Object" numbers as they appear on the Budget Report form. When transferring this information to the Budget Report form, please refer to the instructions on page 11. You should seek assistance from your local finance office to insure that your expenses are properly identified and entered correctly on the Budget Report form on page 8.

100 **Salaries** (Payments are allowed for teacher substitutes only. The payment of salaries and/or stipends to any other personnel will not be allowed in teacher grants. Attach explanation specifying what the released teacher(s) will be doing.)

TOTAL SALARIES $ _____0_____

200 **Employee Benefits** (for Teacher Substitutes, e.g., FICA, etc.)

TOTAL EMPLOYEE BENEFITS $ _____0_____

300 **Purchased Services** (Itemize expenses such as consultant pay, travel, telephone costs, or other purchased services. If you plan to use a consultant, attach a statement of agreement stipulating terms.)

TOTAL PURCHASED SERVICES $ __209.00__

400 **Supplies and Materials** (Itemize and attach)

TOTAL SUPPLIES AND MATERIALS $ _1,209.00_

500 **Capital Outlay** (Itemize and attach)

TOTAL CAPITAL OUTLAY $ __582.00__

TOTAL ESTIMATED COST $ _2,000.00_

PROJECT BUDGET LIMITED TO $2,000

What amount from above will be spent for training or staff development? $ __77.00__

I. Purchased Services

Telephone	$10.00
Speaker Honorarium @ 100.00/day	
Clemson speaker	$100.00
The speaker from SLED is not able to accept an honorarium.	
Travel (from Columbia to Westminster—300 miles)	
(from Clemson to Westminster—40 miles)	
340 miles round trip × .21/miles = $71.40 (round up)	$72.00
Meals for Speakers $18.00/day × 1.5 days	$27.00
Speaker from Columbia Full Day	
Speaker from Clemson Half Day	

TOTAL—Purchased Services $209.00

II. Supplies and Materials

A. Filmstrip—Genetic Engineering		$67.00
Part I. Changing Genetic Messages		
Part II. Issues in Genetic Engineering		
	Packaging and Handling	$8.50

B. Laboratory Supplies

DNA Extraction	
Tissue Homogenizer	$40.00
95% Ethanol (500 ml)	$12.90
Sodium Chloride (500 grams)	$6.50
Sodium Dodecyl Sulfate (SDS) (100 grams)	$17.50
EDTA (100 grams)	$11.90
Microcapillary Pipets	
10 1 (250 pipets)	$25.00
100 1 (250 pipets)	$25.00
DNA Restriction Analysis Kit	
Carolina Biological—Kit #21–1151N	
7 kits @ 57.45/kit	$402.15
$2.43 Ice Pack Charge/Kit	$17.00
DNA Fingerprinting Kit	
Sargent-Welch—Kit #S–18934–07C	
or	
Edvotek—Kit #109	
7 kits @ 55.00/kit	$385.00

TOTAL Laboratory Supplies	$942.95
Shipping and Packaging @ 12%	$113.15

C. Printing of Booklet for Teachers at South Carolina Science Convention $77.00

TOTAL—Supplies and Material $1208.60 (round up) $1,209.00

III. Capital Outlay

Mini-Gel Electrophoresis System	
Carolina Biological—#21–3650N	
4 Systems @ $130.00/system	$520.00
Shipping and Packaging @ 12%	$62.00

TOTAL—Capital Outlay $582.00

This system will be used with the DNA Restriction Analysis Kit and DNA Fingerprinting Kit.

PROJECT TOTAL—Part I, II, III $2,000.00

STATE DEPARTMENT OF EDUCATION
BUDGET REPORT

EDUCATION IMPROVEMENT ACT

MANE OF LEA OR AGENCY:
School District of Oconee County
N. College Street
Walhalla, S.C.   29691

PROGRAM
[X] ORIGINAL   [ ] CHANGE
[ ] AMENDMENT NUMBER

PROJECT NO. [ ][ ][ ]
COUNTY NO. [ ][ ]
DISTRICT NO. [ ]
STATE (1) [1]

SUB PROGRAM [ ]

OBJECT OF EXPENDITURES

FUNCTIONS MAJOR HEADING SERIES	NAME	NO.	SALARIES 100	EMPL'Y BEN 200	PURCHASED SER. 300	SUPP. & MATH 400	CAP. OUTLAY 500	OTHER OBJECTS 600	TRANSFERS 700	TOTALS
INSTRUCTIONAL SERIES		100	0	0		1132 00	582 00	0	0	1714 00
SUPPORT SERVICES SERIES		200			209 00	77 00				286 00
COMMUNITY SERVICES SERIES		300								
NON PROGRAM SERIES		400								
TOTALS			0	0	209 00	1209 00	582 00	0	0	2000 00

SDE 42-061a 00 (This form becomes obsolete 6/30/95.)

EDIT [ ]   SUB PROGRAM [ ]   CLAIM [ ]   DATE: [ ]
SDE USE ONLY

CONTACT PERSON _____

ACTION [ ][ ][ ][ ]

Superintendent's Signature _____   Date _____   Telephone _____

APPENDIX I

Software

Words and Concepts

The title screen of *Words and Concepts* by Laureate Learning Systems presents the teacher with four choices: training, testing, reviewing records, and quitting the program. Option 1, training, presents the activities menu listing the six program selections.

In addition to the vocabulary example mentioned in Chapter 2, the activities menu offers word identification by function. In this program, the student is presented with three pictures and is asked to select one of them based on its function. For example, the student may be asked to "Find the one you wear on your feet" as he or she is shown a picture of a skirt, a blouse, and a pair of shoes. It should be noted that whenever a command is written on the screen, it is also "spoken" by the speech synthesizer program built into the software. Thus, reading skills are not required. This is a very important advantage for at-risk students who may have limited reading abilities.

Whenever a program is selected in this CAI package, the teacher is given the option of changing parameters via a parameters menu. The teacher is allowed to set several parameters. The "interface" option allows the teacher or the student to use different input devices. Selections include the mouse, the arrow keys, a touchwindow, number keys, paddles, joysticks, or trackball.

Pacing can also be varied in this software program. The number of seconds the program waits for the student to respond before moving on to the next presentation may be changed. The response time can be set between 1 and 10 seconds.

Most of the six programs comprising *Words and Concepts* have an errorless learning feature built in. This increases student success and facilitates mastery. This CAI program has three levels of difficulty (discussed in Chapter 2). All three levels provide reinforcement or corrective feedback depending on the student's response.

Option 6 in the parameters menu allows the teacher to determine the number of questions the student must answer correctly in order to proceed to the next skill level. The teacher also has the option of stopping the student on a particular level. The program will start the student on Level 1 and progress to the level specified in Option 5 of the parameters menu. This is important in that the teacher can prevent the student from moving to a skill level for which the student is not prepared.

Another option in the parameters menu allows the teacher to specify the number of questions the student must get correct to end the lesson. The teacher may also decide if the lessons are presented using voice in addition to text, or if the word is to appear with the pictures. This is important for students learning to read. Students can begin with lessons presented in voice and text and then move on to lessons presented only in text. The number of built-in options here indicates that this is a well-written CAI package.

Words and Concepts automatically records student performance and compiles a summary of his or her performance. This summary can be saved on disk or printed. This program also allows the teacher to examine individual word scores for the last skill level on which the student worked. Finally, this software provides the teacher with computerized exams.

Words and Concepts can be used for students at the kindergarten skill level and through adult. Reading proficiency is not required due to the voice option. However, the student must be able to manipulate a mouse or touch screen.

Number Munchers

Number Munchers by Minnesota Educational Computer Corp (MECC) (discussed in Chapter 2) is intended for students aged eight to adult. The student must be able to read the instructions. This software uses a keyboard or a joystick for answer selection. If the keyboard is used, the student must use the keys *i, j, k, l, a* and *z* to move the characters around the screen.

MECC offers a manual to help with the use of *Number Munchers* and gives the teacher a number of options with this program. By pressing CTRL-A, an option menu is presented. Choosing "Game settings" allows the teacher to modify the structure of the games. For example, the teacher may prevent students from playing "Factors" or any of the other games by typing NO in the use column for that particular game. The teacher may also restrict answers to a certain range and specify if the answers are to appear in random order or in increasing order. For example, suppose a student is playing a game where the screen consists of 30 squares, each square containing a different addition problem similar to "10 + 5." The objective is for the Number Muncher to eat the squares that contain problems that give the same answer as the answer at the top of the screen.

Alligator Mix

Alligator Mix by Developmental Learning Materials is another example of mastery practice software. This program helps students increase their skill in addition and subtraction of numbers 0 through 9 by feeding alligators in a swamp. As alligators appear in the swamp, apples with addition and subtraction problems move toward an alligator's mouth. Answers appear in the stomach of the alligator. As the apples approach the alligator, the student must determine if the answer in the alligator is the correct answer for the approaching problem. If it is, the student must open the alligator's mouth by pressing a designated key, allowing the alligator to eat the apple. The alligator lets the student know if the apple was a "good" or "bad" apple (a correct or incorrect answer), or, if the student didn't feed the alligator an apple, that the student should have fed the alligator. Correct and incorrect answers are identified by the sound the program makes when the apple reaches the alligator and by pictures that appear above the alligator's head. As the student improves, more alligators are added to the swamp, increasing the speed of the game. Hits and misses are recorded at the bottom of the screen.

A teacher's manual, worksheets, student record sheets, and flash cards are included with *Alligator Mix*. Also, this CAI program allows the teacher to change several parameters of the game. To change options, press CTRL-P. There are several options that may be modified. For example, pacing is controlled by selecting a number between 1 and 9, to predetermine how long the student has to choose an answer.

The academic level can also be varied. For example, if the teacher selects a problem range of 6, then the problems will contain only the digits 0 through 6. If the selected problem range is 9, then the problems will contain the digits 0 through 9. The teacher also can change the length of a game by the run-time option. For example, if 2 is selected, the game will run for 2 minutes. Games can run between 1 and 5 minutes.

Oregon Trail

Oregon Trail by MECC is a simulation of the pioneers migrating west on the Oregon Trail. Along the way, several participants actively engage in roles that involve deciding what supplies to purchase, when to make camp, when to continue traveling, where to cross rivers, and so on. For example, when starting the program, the student is asked to choose a profession. Choices of professions include a doctor, a carpenter, a farmer, and others. Based on the profession chosen, the student is informed of the amount of money he or she will have for the purchase of supplies.

During the journey, the student is required to make decisions about when to rest, ford rivers, purchase more supplies, hunt, change the speed of travel, start the journey, and change trails. Bad decisions usually result in illness, injury, or possibly death to the character the student is portraying or to a member of the party. The student is rewarded for consistently good decisions by safely completing the journey.

To actually plan and carry out such a major expedition is impossible for most people, due to cost and time requirements, but a simulation, such as *Oregon Trail*, can encourage some of the informal learning that would take place on such an adventure. This simulation would work well with groups of students or an entire class. The students must have reading skills to read the instructions and information presented during the journey. The school version of *Oregon Trail* comes with student handouts and an easy-to-read manual.

Life Skills

Life Skills by Hartley is a simulation package that teaches students several important skills for living in today's society. It consists of 10 different programs, each teaching a new skill. Instruction in life skills of this nature is particularly appropriate for at-risk students.

In addition to "Checking Accounts," and "Comparison Shopping" discussed in Chapter 2, other programs in this simulation package include:

1. "Advertising," which teaches the student how to evaluate advertisements.
2. "Following Directions," where the student practices following directions to complete real-life tasks such as riding subways, using pay phones, operating appliances, and so on.
3. "Interviewing," in which the student practices interviewing skills by examining body language, personal appearance, and other aspects of presenting oneself in an interview.
4. "Using Credit," which teaches the student about budgeting, using credit cards, and paying bills. This type of program can be particularly useful with students who are at-risk.

5. "On the Job," which places the student in the job of store owner and requires him or her to hire employees. In addition to hiring employees, the student learns about proper job behavior, dependability, punctuality, and the like.
6. "Planning a Trip," in which the student learns how to read a map, plan a route which takes into account distance, where to eat, how to pick a hotel and make reservations, and how to travel with children and pets.

Math Blaster Mystery

Math Blaster Mystery by Davidson, examined in Chapter 2, is for ages 10 through adult, and the student needs reading skills to follow the instructions. Furthermore, some versions of this software asks the student to turn the disk over at times during the activities. Therefore, the student needs to be comfortable with the operation of a computer and its disk drives. The software comes with a manual that describes in detail each activity and the skills used on each level in each activity. The manual also includes teaching tips on how to integrate the software into the curriculum.

Math Shop Jr.

Math Shop Jr., by Scholastic, portrays a mall that consists of 10 shops in which the student works. The student can work in one of the shops or all 10 at the same time. Each shop requires a different set of skills, and each customer wants something slightly different. For example, one of the shops is the "Flower Shop." In this shop, customers come in and ask for a certain number of flowers. It is the student's job to choose one number from each of two given lists so that the two numbers equal the number of flowers the customer desires. Flowers are arranged in two rows. The first row contains bunches of 2, 4, and 7 flowers. The second row contains bunches of 1, 4, and 6 flowers. Customers place their order in the order box on the screen. The student fills the order by adding one bunch of flowers from the first row to one bunch from the second row. After the first few customers, a third row of flowers will appear, containing bunches of 3, 5, and 6 flowers. The student will then fill customer orders by adding one bunch of flowers from each of the three rows. This activity develops skills in addition, categorization, and sequential thinking.

Another shop is the "Rug Shop." In this shop, customers order rugs by the square foot. For each problem, the width of the rug is given. The student decides what the length of the rug must be in order to satisfy the customer.

In *Math Shop Jr.*, the student can work against a clock or at his or her own pace. The student must be able to read the instructions for each shop. When the student serves a customer, the program reinforces success by telling the student that he or she did a good job. If the student makes a mistake, the program responds with the instructions for that shop or tells the student to try that same problem again. *Math Shop Jr.* can be used with all ages. The levels of difficulty vary from shop to shop. For example, the flower shop presents simple addition problems, whereas the rug shop requires the student to understand the concepts of area and the skills of multiplication and division.

Math Shop Jr. comes with a manual containing descriptions of each game that include what skills are needed to play the game, the instructions for each game, and suggestions for its use in the classroom. Student worksheets are also included.

Where in the World Is Carmen San Diego?

Carmen San Diego by Broderbund is for all ages but the student must have reading skills to read the cities, clues, and other instructions. As the student gains confidence by solving crimes, he or she rises from a "Rookie" to an "Ace Detective." When the student fails to solve a crime, the program tells the student that he or she worked hard, did a good job, and was very close to solving the crime. The program then encourages the student to keep trying.

Dr. Peet's Talk/Writer

Dr. Peet's Talk/Writer, discussed in Chapter 2, can be modified in a number of ways by the teacher, and the program presents clear instructions to the teacher to facilitate such modification. Another advantage is that the teacher does not need to do all the modifications at once in order for the program to run. The teacher can do a few modifications at a time, as time allows. This software package itself has several modifications built in, including entering the student's name and indicating if the student is visually impaired, menus to help the teacher set up the system for printing, and modification of speech synthesis. Occasionally in speech synthesis, a word is not pronounced correctly. In these cases, the teacher needs to correct this by using the modification option.

APPENDIX II

Software Sources

Apple, Inc.
One Apple Plaza
P.O. Box 9001
Clearwater, FL 34618
1-800-795-1000

Broderbund Software, Inc.
500 Redwood Highway
Novato, CA 94948
800-521-6263

Claris Corporation
5201 Patrick Henry Dr.
Box 58168
Santa Clara, CA 95052
408-727-8227

Davidson and Associates, Inc.
P.O. Box 2961
Torrance, CA 90509
800-545-7677

Edmark Educational Print
and Software Catalog
P.O. Box 3218
Redmond, WA 98073-3218
800-362-2890

Educational Materials for
the Exceptional Student
Gamco Industries, Inc.
P.O. Box 310R23
Big Spring, TX 79721-1911
800-351-1404

Excelsior Software, Inc.
P.O. Box 3416
Greeley, CO 80633
800-473-4572

Hartley Courseware, Inc.
3451 Dunckel Road
Suite 200
Lansing, MI 48911
800-247-1380

IEP
(*Bonanza*! and *Goal Rush*)
Route 671
P.O. Box 546
Fork Union, VA 23055
804-842-2000

IntelliTools
5221 Central Avenue
Suite 205F
Richmond, CA 94804
800-899-6687

kidTECH
4182 Pinewood Lake Dr.
Bakersfield, CA 93309
805-396-8676

Laurate Learning Systems, Inc.
110 East Spring Street
Winooski, VT 05404-1898
800-562-6801

Learning Company
6493 Kaiser Drive
Fremont, CA 94555
800-852-2255

Lotus Developmental
Corporation
55 Cambridge Parkway
Cambridge, MA 02142
617-577-8500

Marblesoft
12301 Central Avenue, NE
Suite 205
Blaine, MN 55434
612-755-1402

MECC Educational Software
6160 Summit Drive North
Minneapolis, MN 55430-4003
800-685-MECC

Microsoft Corp.
1 Microsoft Way
Redmond, WA 98052-6399
800-426-9400

Power Industries LP
37 Walnut Street
Wellesley Hills, MA 02181
800-395-5009

Resource Guide for Persons with
Learning Impairments
National Support Center for Persons
with Disabilities
International Business Machines,
Inc.
P.O. Box 1328
Boca Raton, FL 33429-1328
800-426-4832

R. J. Cooper
24843 Del Prado, Suite 283
Dana Point, CA 92629
714-240-1912

SAMS
Division of Prentice Hall Computer
Publishing
11711 North College
Carmel, IN 46032

Scholastic, Inc.
P.O. Box 7502
2391 E. McCardy St.
Jefferson City, MO 65102
314-636-5271

Special Education Management
System (SEMS)
Eutactics, Inc.
21 Salt Island Road
Gloucester, MA 01930
800-323-7077

Special Times
Cambridge Development
Laboratory, Inc.
86 West Street
Waltham, MA 02154
800-637-0047

Springboard Software, Inc.
7808 Creekridge Circle
Minneapolis, MN 55435
612-944-3915

SRA, a Division of MacMillian,
MacGraw-Hill
(software formerly owned by
Developmental Learning Materials)
P.O. Box 543
860 Taylor Station Road
Blacklick, OH 43004
800-843-8855

Sunburst Communications
101 Castleton Street
P.O. Box 100
Pleasantville, NY 10570-0100
800-321-7511

Tom Snyder Productions, Inc.
Watertown, MA
617-926-6000

Wordperfect, Inc.
1555 N. Technology Way
Orem, UT 84057-2399
801-225-5000

APPENDIX **III**

Assistive Technology

Earlier in this book we mentioned several pieces of equipment that could be considered assistive or adaptive technology. This equipment included touch screens, mice, and special keyboards such as *Muppet Keys* and *IntelliKeys*. Although a detailed description of assistive technology is beyond the scope of this book, there are several we wish to mention. Here we will review several other assistive technology devices for students with more severe disabilities. We feel that this type of technology is important in that not only does it assist students with disabilities to participate in class but students without disabilities may also enjoy using this technology.

The types of assistive technology that we will examine include speech recognition systems, switching systems, joysticks, touch tablets, screen magnification systems, and braille access systems.

Speech Recognition Systems

Speech recognition systems are the opposite of speech synthesizers, such as the Echo series (discussed in Chapter 3). The goal of speech recognition systems is for the computer to recognize continuous human speech and to act on spoken commands. Unfortunately, human speech has numerous variabilities and complexities of semantics, all of which can cause problems for speech recognition systems.

The current technology allows for these systems to recognize discretely spoken words if they are separated by a pause. Therefore, the user must carefully enunciate each word or command. When commands are spoken in this manner, speech recognition systems give a 60 to 90 percent accuracy rate (Church & Glennen, 1992). Examples of speech recognition systems include Voice Connection's *Introvoice V, VI*, and *Micro Introvoicer* for IBM and IBM compatible computers; Covox, Inc.'s *Voice Master* for Apple II series computers; and Dragon System's *DragonDictate* available for IBM and IBM compatible computers. These systems may be integrated into a computer system using an interface card, special software, and a headset.

With most of the previously mentioned systems, the user must train the computer to recognize his or her voice. This is done by repeating a particular word several times and allowing the computer to analyze it. Therefore, developing just a 100-word vocabulary may take hours. Furthermore, the computer is trained only for that particular person. An exception to this is the speech recognition system *DragonDictate*. This particular system incorporates phonetic models to use in speech recognition. By doing this, *DragonDictate* relieves the user from having to train the speech recognition system with new words. One advantage, therefore, is that the *DragonDictate* system can be used by several people.

Switching Systems

A switch is a device similar to a light switch—it is either open or closed—controlling the flow of electricity. Students with severe motor control problems can use switches to operate computers, toys, and communication devices. For example, switches may be used for game access or as a substitute keyboard.

Using a switch with a computer for game access usually requires a *game I/O switch interface*. This interface is a box-like device that is physically interposed between the computer and the switch. Numerous companies offer switch interfaces for game I/O access.

Single-, dual-, and multiple-switch access methods have been designed to be used in place of a standard keyboard. When switches are used in place of a keyboard, a keyboard emulator is required. The emulator is a software program that translates information from the switches to the computer so that the computer thinks the information is coming from a keyboard.

Joysticks

Joysticks are often used with computer games, graphing and educational programs. A joystick is a stationary box with a stick that moves in two directions. Any movement of the stick results in the x,y coordinates of the position being sent to the computer. Modified joysticks are available for students who are physically disabled. For example, KY Enterprise has a mouth-operated joystick. Also, Lovejoy Electronics produces a light-activated joystick emulator (to use with a pen light mounted on the student's head) for the Apple II series and IBM and IBM compatible computers. This light-activated device, as far as the computer is concerned, acts like a joystick.

Touch Tablets

Touch tablets are similar to touch screens (discussed in Chapter 3) except that they are a flat surface that can be placed on a table, on a desk, or on a student's lap. Touch tablets are plastic membranes that sense the position of a pointer or a finger on the surface. These devices can replace a mouse or a keyboard and are produced by several companies. For example, Koala Technology has a *Koala Pad* for Apple II series and IBM and IBM compatible computers. MicroTouch produces *UnMouse* for Macintosh series, IBM, and IBM compatible computers. Depending on the make of the computer, special software may be needed to use a touch tablet.

Screen Magnification Systems

The devices mentioned thus far are for input of information into the computer. A screen magnification system is for output of information from the computer to a person. These systems are usually used for students who are visually impaired. Depending on the system, characters can be magnified from 2 to 15 times their normal size (Church & Glennen, 1992). Screen magnification systems can be hardware (equipment that is attached to the monitor or computer), software, or a combination of the two.

The simplest and cheapest way to magnify the computer screen is by the use of a fresnel lens, which is basically an adjustable lens that can be attached to any standard computer monitor. One example of a fresnel lens is *Compu-Lenz,* produced by AbleTech Connection, for use with any computer monitor.

For some students, the fresnel lens may not give enough magnification. In these cases, the next step to consider is specialized software. This type of software not only allows users to choose the magnification size but it also allows him or her to zoom and magnify part or all of the computer screen. Most of these software packages cannot be used with all computers and graphics programs. So this should be checked before purchasing a software-based magnification system. Examples of this type of software include *inLarger* by Berkeley System for Macintosh series computers and *MAGic* and *MAGic Deluxe* produced by Microsystems Software for IBM and IBM compatible computers.

Braille Access Systems

Braille is a system of writing for the blind that consists of characters represented by patterns of raised dots. Braille access systems allow students with visual impairments access to computer systems. These systems include devices such as braille-style keyboards, terminals, speech synthesizers, and braille printers.

For a computer to accept braille input and produce braille output requires a combination of software and hardware that acts as a translator between the student using braille and the computer. Since the input and output must go through this translator, computers with braille access systems are slower than computers without these systems.

Conclusion

In this appendix, we have touched on the most common assistive technology that was not covered earlier in the book. Most of the devices discussed can be found or ordered at a retail computer store. We hope that we have given you an idea of the types of devices that are available for students with physical disabilities to aid them in the use of computers. For those of you who would like more detail on this topic, we suggest the book by Church and Glennen (1992).

References

Carey, D. M., & Sale, P. (1994). Notebook Computers Increase Communication. *Teaching Exceptional Children*, 27(1), 62–69.

Church, G., & Glennen, S. (1992). *The Handbook of Assistive Technology*. San Diego, CA: Singular Publishing.

Lewis, R. (1993). *Special Education Technology Classroom Applications*. Pacific Grove, CA: Brooks/Cole.

Index